# Gothic
### REVIVAL

MEGAN ALDRICH

# Gothic
## REVIVAL

Phaidon Press Ltd
Regent's Wharf
All Saints Street
London N1 9PA

First published 1994
Reprinted 1997
© Phaidon Press Limited

ISBN 0 7148 2886 6 (Hb)
ISBN 0 7148 3631 1 (Pb)

Printed in Hong Kong

*Endpapers: A modern
reproduction by Cole & Son
of a wallpaper first produced
for Naunton Court,
Somerset, in 1829. With its
three-dimensional traceried
effect, it is typical of the
wallpaper and textile
designs favoured by Gothic
Revivalists in the 1820s
and 30s.*

*Half-title page: Design
for Window Drapery by
Thomas Sheraton, 1807.
While Sheraton's name is
normally associated with
classicism in design, he could
accommodate those with a
taste for the Gothic, as seen
in this illustration from his*
Encyclopedia *of designs.*

*Facing Title page:
Illustration of the
'Extravagant Style' of
Modern Gothic Furniture
and Decoration by*

*A W N Pugin, published in*
The True Principles of
Pointed or Christian
Architecture, *1841. In this
plate, Pugin illustrated a
number of early nineteenth-
century Gothic design
features that he later came
to detest, such as the idea
of elaborate sham fan and
pendant vaults applied
purely for decorative
purposes or the use of flying
buttresses taken from
cathedral architecture to
'support' the base of a small
occasional table.*

*Title page: Polychromed
and gilt cabinet on a
stand, 1858, designed
by William Burges and
made by Harland and
Fisher of London;
paintings by E J Poynter.
Since the discovery that
medieval furniture had
been richly painted,
designers like Burges tried
to revive this type of
decoration in their Gothic
Revival furniture.*

*Page 5 opposite: Design for
a wallpaper, A W N Pugin,
1847. This design for the
Palace of Westminster was
derived from Italian textiles
of the fifteenth and sixteenth
centuries.*

*Page 6: A detail from the
Church of St Giles, Cheadle,
Staffordshire, A W N Pugin,
1841–6. In the 1840s Pugin
used 'polychromy' in deep
colours and gilt to build up
layers of pattern.*

*Contents page:
Designs for garden
structures, published in
William Halfpenny's*
Rural Architecture in the
Gothick Taste, *1752. Such
structures would be used in
a landscape garden to create
a 'picturesque' view.*

# Contents

This book examines the attitudes and individuals that shaped the Gothic Revival, from its beginnings in the early eighteenth century to its decline as an active architectural tradition at the close of the nineteenth century. In terms of existing buildings, the nineteenth century predominates. Nonetheless, the eighteenth century offers a surprising number of important examples of Gothic Revival design, which have received less attention than they deserve in accounts so far.

The phenomenon of the Gothic Revival is of great interest to historians and to enthusiasts of architecture and design because of its links with other aspects of cultural life, namely, literature, scholarship and collecting. These intellectual activities gave impetus to those who chose the Gothic as a style for their houses or furnishings. Despite its distinctive appearance, it was seldom chosen purely for its visual and aesthetic properties. The Gothic generated literature, theory and debate about its forms, its symbolism and its origins, and thus it became the chosen style for thinking people who wished to associate themselves with the past, with scholarship, or with the unusual, the exotic, and the remote.

During the eighteenth century the typical patron of Gothic Revival architecture was an aristocratic gentleman or lady with antiquarian leanings and the means to build ornamental garden structures or to alter a country house. After 1800 the Gothic attracted more attention and became more widely used, becoming an option for middle-class house-builders with romantic inclinations. Throughout the nineteenth century, 'prodigy' houses in the Gothic style were built for wealthy owners who wanted to associate themselves with the medieval past, while the Gothic remained an option used by the discerning bourgeoisie – the same clientele who despised most of the objects shown in the Great Exhibition of 1851 for their excessive eclecticism and lack of coherence in design. The Gothic style was often the choice of those with intellectual or artistic leanings.

The Gothic Revival was undoubtedly a design phenomenon that reached its widest extent in the English-speaking world. It was also influential in Germany and France during the nineteenth century and made its appearance in other European countries. The European dimension to the Gothic Revival is relatively little-known at present, aside from the career of the French architect Viollet-le-Duc, who was widely influential both in France and in Britain. A thorough study of the Gothic Revival in Continental Europe would deepen our understanding of this fascinating chapter in intellectual and design history.

This book focuses on the Gothic style in domestic architecture, from country houses to cottages. Earlier books on the Gothic Revival have concentrated on ecclesiastical and public architecture in the nineteenth century. However, until the rebuilding of the Palace of Westminster, destroyed in a fire of 1834, the most widespread and the most important Gothic Revival monuments were houses, rather than churches or public buildings. Domestic architecture of the Gothic Revival has received less attention than it deserves, and it is this shortfall that this book is intended to address.

*Alscot Park, Warwickshire, c1750–64. The façade owes something to the designs published by Batty Langley in 1741–2 through its reliance upon the ogee arch for doors, windows and tracery.*

The Annunciation *by the Master of Flemalle, c1430. Here the setting has been created by means of a vaulted space with rich, Late Gothic detailing such as battlements, gables and pinnacles. The use of Gothic architecture in Northern Europe overlapped the Renaissance period.*

In that year were seen for the first time at Chartres the faithful harnessed to carts, laden with stones, timbers, corn and whatever might be needed for the work of building the cathedral, the towers of which rose like magic into the heavens... Men and women could be seen dragging heavy loads through mire and marsh, praising in song the miracle which God was performing before their eyes. *Robert de Mont-Saint-Michel (1144)*

*The north rose window, Cathedral of Chartres, France, c1220–40. Chartres Cathedral is extraordinary for the amount of original stained glass that it contains. The north and south transepts, built in the thirteenth century, were originally designed to have a rose window surmounting a cluster of five lancets, as seen here. The theme of the north rose window (c1220–40) is the Patriarchs and Prophets of the Old Testament, which is echoed in the exterior sculpture of the north portal.*

Understanding the revival of a past style involves a double leap of the imagination, first to comprehend the characteristics and associations of the style which was revived, and second to determine why that style should be seen as evocative and appropriate within a different age and context. Such is the case with the Gothic Revival, which spanned a period of over 150 years during the eighteenth and nineteenth centuries.

A variety of types of medieval architecture served as sources for the Gothic Revival, ranging from fortified castle residences to ruined abbeys. However, the primary source of inspiration was Gothic architecture, which was developed in northern France in the middle of the twelfth century and remained in use until the beginning of the sixteenth century. The Gothic style transformed the classical grammar of columns, lintels, pediments and round arches into a visual language of slender colonettes, buttresses, pointed arches and vaulting, giving rise to vast interior spaces.

One of the most eloquent and widely read champions of Gothic architecture during the nineteenth century was the English art critic John Ruskin. We can look to Ruskin for an explanation of why the style was of such interest to designers working in the modern era. In his important book *The Stones of Venice* (1853), Ruskin devoted a chapter to 'The Nature of Gothic', in which he praised Gothic architecture for 'the magnificent science of its structure, and the sacredness of its expression.' What fascinated Ruskin and his contemporaries was not only the extraordinary feats of engineering achieved by the great Gothic masons, but also the spirituality of Gothic design, which struck a chord at a time when the effects of industrialization and the materialism of Western culture were subjects of widespread concern.

Ruskin praised the freedom with which craftsmen worked in the Gothic age, noting the great variations in structure and ornamentation seen when comparing Gothic buildings of different periods and regions. He proposed that this perceived freedom resulted in an art that was vibrant and reflected the individuality of each craftsman, unlike the dull, repetitive quality of factory-produced objects after the Industrial Revolution. *The Stones of Venice* also paid tribute to the adaptability of the Gothic style:

In The Stones of Venice
(1853), the English art critic
John Ruskin illustrated
examples of Venetian
medieval architecture whose
design he admired. This
illustration shows the ogeed
windows of the thirteenth-
century Casa Falier on the
Grand Canal.

Windows with tall ogee
arches and cusping from
the Priuli Palace, of the
late fourteenth century,
illustrated in The Stones
of Venice. Ruskin was
fascinated by the way
Eastern and Western
architectural elements were
mixed in medieval Venice.

*For in one point of view Gothic is not only the
best, but the only rational architecture, as being
that which can fit itself most easily to all
services, vulgar or noble.*

The Gothic was an ecclesiastical style best
suited to churches and cathedrals, but the
modular nature of Gothic ornament and
structure meant it could be scaled down
and adapted to humbler buildings.

Ruskin contrasted the organic nature
of the style with the formal symmetry of
classically inspired architecture:

*And it is one of the chief virtues of the Gothic
builders, that they never suffered ideas of outside
symmetries and consistencies to interfere with
the real use and value of what they did. If they
wanted a window, they opened one; a room,
they added one; a buttress, they built one;
utterly regardless of any established
conventionalities of external appearance.*

The asymmetry and variety of forms
found within Gothic architecture was seen
by Ruskin as evidence of 'honesty' of
design and construction, in contrast to

the artificial regularity of classical design.

The Gothic age was a great period of
northern European civilization, in which
important developments were achieved in
the fields of architecture, sculpture and
manuscript illumination, as well as literature,
theology and philosophy. However, when
the adjective 'Gothic' was first applied to
medieval architecture in the seventeenth
century, it was used as a term of disparage-
ment by writers who considered the Goths
to be the barbarian peoples of northern
Europe who destroyed classical civilization,
leading to the 'Dark Ages' of the early
medieval period. Italian writers in the
Renaissance period, who were steeped in
the classical tradition, disliked the Gothic
because it failed to observe classical rules
and proportions of building.

At the beginning of the seventeenth
century Gothic art was considered to be
barbaric and primitive. Sir Henry Wotton,
an admirer of Rubens, wrote in 1624 of
'the natural imbecility of the sharp angle',
referring to the pointed arch. Later in the
century Sir Christopher Wren, the scientist
and architect to Charles II, observed:

*A detail of the choir transept at Salisbury Cathedral (completed by 1258). Like many Gothic cathedrals, Salisbury has an extra transept towards the east of the choir. Late in the fourteenth century, a period of great innovation in English vaulting, the inverted 'strainer' arches seen here were added to reinforce the vaulting of the choir crossing, which was under pressure. The most famous examples of 'strainer' arches can be seen at Wells Cathedral in Somerset, dating from about 1340.*

*Fan vaulting of the south range of the cloister of Gloucester Cathedral, c1350–64. These are the earliest known fan vaults, and they mark the transition from Decorated to Perpendicular Gothic in England. Seen on the right-hand side of this view are built-in carrels, or stalls, where monks could sit to study and reflect.*

*Opposite: The beautiful fan-like shapes of the vaulting in Gloucester Cathedral were created by spreading out the ribs before they reached the roof. The resulting 'fans' were used by masons as a way of displaying carved tracery, while the flat roof surface between the vaults was decorated with rosettes.*

*The Goths and Vandals, having demolished the Greek and Roman architecture, introduced in its stead a certain fantastical and licentious manner of building which we have since called modern or Gothic – of the greatest industry and expressive carving, full of fret and lamentable imagery, sparing neither pains nor cost.*

When the old Gothic Cathedral of St Paul in London was badly damaged in the Great Fire of 1666, Wren seized the opportunity to rebuild it in a classicizing Baroque style. However, by the middle of the seventeenth century an appreciation of the Gothic was developing. The English diarist and traveller John Evelyn, for example, remarked favourably upon the architecture of the Gothic church at Haarlem during a trip to the Netherlands in 1641. In 1654, he went so far as to describe York Minster as 'a most entire and magnificent piece of Gotic [Gothic] architecture.' By the end of the seventeenth century, serious study of Gothic architecture had begun amongst antiquarians and scholars.

The visual characteristics of Gothic art include the use of a vivid programme of colour, known as polychromy, in both the plastic and the pictorial arts and, generally speaking, the use of stylized forms arranged in narrative fashion. Gothic art nearly always has a story to tell relating to the Christian faith, the Bible being its central source of inspiration. Gothic art instructed people by visual means in the Christian faith at a time when few could read, and Gothic architecture overpowered and dwarfed the individual to impress upon him the power of God, in whose 'house' he stood while attending Mass. The focal point of Gothic art was the cathedral, the physical manifestation of the medieval Christian faith.

Echoing Ruskin's remark on the sacredness of the Gothic style, the German scholar Hans Jantzen has termed the Gothic 'the sacred style of Europe'. The Gothic

*Winchester Cathedral, in a watercolour by John Buckler, 1801. Originally dating from the Norman period, Winchester's nave was remodelled in the Perpendicular Gothic style during the final quarter of the fourteenth century. The large Perpendicular west window, seen here, was installed at the same date.*

*Wells Cathedral, in an early nineteenth-century watercolour by John Buckler. The main body of the cathedral was consecrated in 1239, but important additions in the Decorated Gothic style were constructed in the fourteenth century. These included the east part of the choir, the Lady Chapel, the crossing tower and the polygonal Chapter House, visible here in front of the flying buttresses.*

cathedral represented, literally, the 'house of God' on earth, and its construction – often involving the whole community – was regarded as a fervent expression of faith. This is eloquently described by Robert de Mont-Saint-Michel in his account of the building of Chartres Cathedral, in which he described men and women drawing carts to transport the stone. In the towers of Laon Cathedral in Normandy, two oxen were carved to represent the supposedly miraculous appearance of these beasts to pull the stone-laden carts.

The design of the great Gothic churches was highly symbolic. They took the form of the Cross upon which Christ was crucified and pointed to the east, towards Jerusalem. Some scholars have suggested that the pointed arch, the cusp and other Gothic features were borrowed from Islamic architecture which the early Crusaders would have seen in the Holy Land. Because it pointed towards Jerusalem, the holiest area of the church was in the east, which contained the altar. Here the symbolic sacrifice of the Mass took place during which the wafer and wine were miraculously 'transformed' into the body and blood of Christ.

Above all, Gothic design exploited the use of light in architecture through the opening up of wall surfaces by means of vaulting. Large areas of the wall could be pierced and glazed with beautiful coloured glass (illustrating religious subjects), allowing the worshipper to experience physical and spiritual 'illumination' simultaneously. The symbolic power of light was discussed in the twelfth-century writings of the Abbot Suger of St Denis in France, who noted that the glow of stained glass windows symbolized

heavenly spiritual light. The idea that physical and spiritual levels of reality should be present at the same time is a central concept to the Gothic age.

The French Gothic Revival architect and theorist, Eugène Viollet-le-Duc, discussed the emotional power of architecture in his famous *Entretiens*, or 'Lectures', of 1863. He described sitting in Notre Dame Cathedral as a young boy and being overcome by the experience of hearing the organ and seeing the glow of the stained glass, which seemed to vibrate with the music. In England, A W N Pugin was attracted to the richness of Gothic architecture and the forms of Catholic worship of the English Middle Ages. His biographer and contemporary Benjamin Ferrey tells us:

*Pugin always expressed his unmitigated disgust at the cold and sterile forms of the Scotch (Presbyterian) Church; and the moment he broke loose from the trammels imposed upon him by his mother, he rushed into the arms of a church which pompous by its ceremonies was attractive to his imaginative mind.*

The Gothic age was an age of faith, not empiricism. Mystery was, from the beginning, an important part of worship in the great Gothic cathedrals. The congregation stood in the nave of the cathedral, and until the thirteenth century the priests and altar were hidden from view during the Eucharist. Thereafter they were glimpsed at a distance through screens that marked off the easternmost area of the church. The miracle of Transubstantiation took place out of sight, but within the presence of the worshippers. The Gothic style, from its beginnings in

*Whitby Abbey in Yorkshire (c1175–1200): one of a group of northern English and Scottish abbeys and minsters built in the new Gothic style during the final quarter of the twelfth century. It is generally thought that Whitby was directly inspired by nearby Ripon Minster. Despite the prevalence here of the sharply pointed arches typical of Early English Gothic, some round-headed arches in the Romanesque style are also visible.*

the Middle Ages, was associated with the mysterious, with that which is present in Nature yet also above and beyond it, and Gothic cathedrals were physical manifestations of this two-tiered concept of reality.

The idea that reality might have several layers was central to much literature of the Gothic Revival. The Irish author Bram Stoker wrote his famous Gothic novel *Dracula* in 1892, in which his principal character, the Dutch Professor Van Helsing, chastized his English pupil, Dr John Seward, for failing to recognize the marks of the vampire (signifying another reality) on his patient:

*You do not let your eyes see nor your ears hear, and that which is outside your daily life is not of account to you. Do you not think that there are things which you cannot understand, and yet which are; that some people see things that others cannot?…Ah, it is the fault of our science that it wants to explain all; and if it explain not, then it says there is nothing to explain.*

For the supernatural character of Count Dracula, the only possible residence was an enormous, partly ruined medieval castle set on a rocky outcrop in almost impenetrable forest in the wild mountains of Transylvania. When Dracula decided to buy a house in England, his agent selected one in a remote location, surrounded by trees:

*Carfax, no doubt a corruption of the old Quatre Face…The house is very large and of*

Moonlight, *by Sebastian Pether, 1841. The ruined abbeys left behind after the English Reformation were frequently the subject of the Romantic painters of the nineteenth century. Pether portrays the Gothic ruins of an abbey in the foreground with a Gothic castle on the left. The architecture is almost certainly a fantasy, as is the rocky, wild-looking landscape.*

*all periods back, I should say, to medieval times, for one part is of stone immensely thick, with only a few windows high up and heavily barred with iron. It looks like part of a keep, and is close to an old chapel or church.*

A setting deep in the 'mists of time' was an essential ingredient of the Gothic novel, which arose from the fertile imagination of Horace Walpole in the 1760s as a genre distinct from the rational, moralizing tone of much eighteenth-century literature. Walpole, who built a pioneering house in the Gothic style, remarked that one needed taste to appreciate classical art but passion to appreciate the Gothic.

It is not surprising that the most rational of novelists, Jane Austen, should have parodied the naivety and swooning sensibilities of certain Gothic heroines in *Northanger Abbey*, which she began writing in 1798. The 'ignorant and uninformed' Catherine failed to distinguish between the fantastic happenings within the Gothic novels she loved to read (especially those by Ann Radcliffe, written in the 1790s) and the realistic possibilities of life in England at the opening of the nineteenth century. In *Northanger Abbey*, Catherine's reaction upon being invited to stay with her friends, the Tilneys, at the abbey, was one of delight:

*Her passion for ancient edifices was next in degree to her passion for Henry Tilney – and*

*castles and abbeys made usually the charm of
those reveries which his image did not fill.
To see and explore either the ramparts and
keep of the one, or the cloisters of the other,
had been for many weeks a darling wish,
though to be more than the visitor of an hour,
had seemed too nearly impossible for desire.
And yet, this was to happen. With all the
chances against her of house, hall, place,
park, court and cottage, Northanger turned
up an abbey, and she was to be its inhabitant.
Its long, damp passages, its narrow cells
and ruined chapel, were to be within her
daily reach, and she could not entirely
subdue the hope of some traditional legends,
some awful memorials of an injured and
ill-fated nun.*

Catherine's adventures at the abbey, the
results of her confusing everyday reality with
the reality in her imagination, were gently
censured by the character Henry Tilney,
who was probably expressing the views of
Jane Austen herself:

*The person, be it gentleman or lady, who has
not pleasure in a good novel, must be intolerably
stupid. I have read all Mrs Radcliffe's works,
and most of them with great pleasure. The
Mysteries of Udolpho, when I had once begun
it, I could not lay down again; I remember
finishing it in two days – my hair standing on
end the whole time.*

However, Henry warned Catherine not to
become too absorbed in the world of the
Gothic imagination. While Jane Austen's
reasoned views represented the majority
opinion in the eighteenth century, Bram
Stoker's characters in *Dracula*, who were

forced to acknowledge the power of another
world outside their daily lives, represent the
more complex views that developed in the
nineteenth century.

The Gothic Revival was of great importance in the development of architecture and
design of the modern period. It was not until
the deliberate revival of medieval forms of
architecture began during the eighteenth
century that the long period of dominance
of classicism in design was to end. During
the second half of the eighteenth century,
the adoption of a particular style became a
matter of informed choice, and the use of the
Gothic style meant that a certain statement
was being made by the patron or architect.
By ending the dominance of classicism in
domestic architecture, the Gothic Revival
ushered in an era where the use of varied
styles in architecture and design was,
and still is, a subject of lively debate. With
the eighteenth century concept of the
Picturesque, a development in landscape
design, came the fashion for using a range of
unusual or exotic styles.

Early in the nineteenth century, the
Gothic began to assume an increasingly
prominent role in England. It was used by
owners of real medieval manors and castles
as the appropriate style for refurbishments,
or by patrons who wished to establish a
link with the medieval past, and hence
English antiquity. The association of Gothic
architecture at this time with dramatic or
imposing natural settings linked it firmly
to the development of the Romantic
Movement.

In the 1820s and 30s, the Gothic style
became more archaeological in character as
owners of medieval houses sought furnishings

*An illustration of the Coronation Banquet of James II, Westminster Hall, London, 1685. Originally the Great Hall of the Norman kings, Westminster Hall received an enormous hammerbeam roof c1399 under the supervision of the architect Henry Yevele. This system of construction resembling vaulting in wood, may have been derived from shipbuilding techniques.*

based upon genuine medieval sources, and earlier Gothic Revival structures began to be criticized for their lack of fidelity to ancient models.

This shift in attitude ushered in the Gothic of the 1840s, which was dominated by A W N Pugin, who promoted a new richness and authentic medievalism even in relatively modest domestic architecture. Thanks partly to his efforts, Gothic had become the most important of revived styles of architecture in Europe by the middle of the nineteenth century. After Pugin's premature death in 1852, his followers continued working more or less according to his ideas during the 1850s and 60s. However, by the early 1860s Gothic Revival design began to diverge into two distinct streams.

The first of these might be considered as the avant-garde of Gothic Revival design, which evolved into the Aesthetic Movement and the Arts and Crafts Movement in Britain, and contributed towards Art Nouveau and Surrealism on the Continent. By doing so, this avant-garde stream was to lose its Gothic characteristics. The second stream of Gothic Revival design, later in the nineteenth century, saw the building of a number of spectacular houses and castles for the very wealthy. These residences were often theatrical in character, resembling stage sets built for eccentric, if erudite, owners. This type of Gothic was to go out of fashion early in the twentieth century with the advent of 'modernism' and the rejection of historical styles as the basis for design.

Medieval Gothic architecture developed as an ecclesiastical building style whose greatest achievements were the creation of enormous Gothic cathedrals in stone. As the seats of bishops, the great medieval cathedrals were often located in market

*A detail of sculpture in the north portal, Chartres Cathedral, c1204–24. Sculpture was an important part of the decoration of a cathedral. In the centre is the figure of John the Baptist, who carries the lamb symbolizing the forthcoming sacrifice of Christ. While the figurative style of the sculpture is not as naturalistic as that of the slightly later south portal, nonetheless the increasing variation in the patterns of drapery, hair and attitudes of the figures anticipates the naturalism of the High Gothic sculpture of the thirteenth century.*

*Opposite: The nave from the south aisle, Durham Cathedral, Co Durham, c1115–30. The massive, fortress-like architecture of the Romanesque cathedral at Durham was the work of Norman architects. However, the nave is unusual in that it contains the earliest surviving pointed rib vault, a feature which was to become central to the Gothic style. The use of the pointed arch here was probably due to technical difficulties with the vaulting, since the other nave features – round arches, massive piers and geometric mouldings – are thoroughly Romanesque.*

towns and accommodated increasingly large local populations of worshippers, as well as pilgrims. Until the nineteenth century, the great Gothic cathedrals contained the largest interior spaces man was capable of creating.

Gothic architecture began to evolve in northern France during the twelfth century, a period of great cultural activity, from Romanesque architecture. As its name implies, the Romanesque was based upon ancient Roman principles of building, with an emphasis upon the basilica plan (a central nave with two side aisles), the round-headed arch, and, occasionally, the use of the dome

to create large interior spaces. Many of the Romanesque churches in France display these characteristics, and the majority of them lie in the south of France, where classical remains from antiquity were available for study. Germany and Italy, where there were many antique remains, were also regions rich in Romanesque architecture. The Gothic was introduced more slowly in these areas.

In England the term 'Norman' signifies Romanesque, as it was recognized that the style had been promoted, if not introduced, by the Normans at the time of the Conquest. The twelfth-century church of St Bartholomew the Great in London is an example of the style, where the nave relies upon round-headed arches, formed from the arc of a circle, which spring from the squat capitals of sturdy piers. In Romanesque architecture, the stone mass of the wall is load-bearing, and large areas of masonry are necessary for structural stability. In addition, the ornamental vocabulary of the Romanesque features bands of simple geometrical ornament, as seen in the early twelfth-century nave of Durham Cathedral. Designed in the Romanesque style, with ornament taken from nature, it is executed in a highly stylized fashion.

Gothic architecture represents a strong contrast. From the massive, severe-looking churches of the Romanesque developed the elegant, soaring Gothic cathedrals. The remarkable Abbot Suger, at the abbey church of St Denis to the north of Paris, engaged masons to create what is recognized as the earliest Gothic structure in the world, the choir, or east end, of St Denis during the 1140s. The choir had pointed arches, the trademark of the Gothic style.

*The west portal of Rheims Cathedral, Picardy, France, c1230–60. The construction of the present-day cathedral began in 1211 after a fire destroyed the earlier building. Its façade has a distinctive design of three deeply recessed portals, creating a powerful effect of dark and light, surmounted by three sharply pointed gables with sculptural decoration. Rheims offers an impressive example of the new Rayonnant Gothic that was to become widespread throughout France.*

During the twelfth century, masons in northern France had begun to experiment with breaking the continuous arc of a circle, the basis of the round arch, into two intersecting arcs, thereby creating a pointed arch. The result was a modular building system that is highly flexible, as the pointed arch can be widened or narrowed at will to accommodate the width of the bays beneath it.

Gothic cathedral interiors are organized around a system of colonettes, or slender columns, which are usually grouped in clusters. These colonettes rise continuously from the nave piers to the springing of the vaulted ceiling, marking out the lines of support of the roof. Visually, the sensation created is one of soaring verticals repeated at regular intervals down the length of the church. The weight of the building is concentrated onto the load-bearing ribs, which support the roof; the masonry walls

and ceiling are used not for support, but to keep out the weather and to stabilize the vaulted structure. This represents a much more sophisticated system of architectural design than that of the Romanesque, and it was to become the basis for construction of the twentieth-century 'skyscraper'. The result of this revolution in architecture, whereby vaulting could be used to hold up the roof, was that the wall could be cut away to a great extent. The resulting space was used to exploit the properties of light in architecture for its decorative and symbolic possibilities. Magnificent stained glass windows increasingly occupied the spaces between the colonettes of the nave, giving the effect of light-filled glass walls between the vertical supports, and depicting Christian images.

The nave of York Minster, completed in the fourteenth century, is an example of the fully developed Gothic style in Britain. The sharply pointed arches of its nave arcade soar to over half the height of the ceiling above, creating an impression of vast unbroken space. The walls appear weightless, as if they are thin membranes pierced by light.

Gothic architecture quickly spread from northern France to England, as there were close ties between the two countries during the Middle Ages. French and English Gothic developed in different directions, each displaying characteristic phases in this development. Whereas French Gothic cathedrals are distinctive for their great height, with the stressing of vertical elements in the architecture, English masons tended to build Gothic cathedrals of enormous length and emphasized horizontal mouldings

*A German stained glass window from Cologne, c1380. The presence of cusped gables in the architectural canopy here signals the influence of the French Gothic style, used widely in late medieval decorative art on the Continent. The introduction of colours such as pink and green in large areas is typical of Late Gothic glass. The classic Early Gothic windows of the thirteenth century used a palette of deep blue and red, with white, yellow and other colours used sparingly.*

*The Upper Chapel at La Sainte Chapelle, Paris, 1243–8, probably designed by Pierre de Montreuil and built for the sainted Louis IX of France. This is the classic example of French Rayonnant, or radiating, Gothic. Here the walls have been almost entirely filled in with panels of stained glass, while the ribs of the vaulting radiate from the centre of the ceiling down to the floor.*

in their design. This can be seen in the verticality of the façade of Amiens Cathedral, which presents a contrast to the horizontal emphasis of the façade of Exeter Cathedral.

The most famous successor to the Gothic church at St Denis was the Cathedral at Chartres, whose west façade (entrance front) contains early Gothic portal sculpture and a rose window inspired by that at St Denis. The façade is massive with large areas of masonry when compared to later Gothic façades such as that of the Cathedral at Rheims. Nonetheless, it is characteristic of Gothic with its pointed arches, deep cutting into the wall surface for portals and windows, and large rose window above the ground storey.

The classic French 'Early Gothic' style can be seen at Laon Cathedral in Normandy. The organization of the façade takes the form of a triple-arched portal surmounted by a large rose window where the stone tracery appears to radiate from its centre like the petals of a flower. At the top are twin towers with tall, narrow, pointed openings. Early Gothic is characterized by relatively large areas of wall mass, with compact stepped buttresses, and a simple geometric system of arranging the architectural elements, both inside and out.

Rayonnant, or 'radiating' Gothic, developed in France during the third quarter of the thirteenth century and can be seen again at St Denis, where the nave was reconstructed. The Rayonnant style placed great emphasis on opening up the wall surface to contain large areas of stained glass. The interiors have a system of ribs that seem to radiate from the vaulting of the roof down to the floor in an uninterrupted flowing rhythm. A classic example of the style is La Sainte Chapelle in Paris, a richly decorated private chapel built for Louis IX (St Louis) around the middle of the thirteenth century.

In the fifteenth century, in part responding to the increasing elaboration of English Gothic, a new and more elaborately decorated form of French Gothic made its appearance. This became known as Flamboyant, or 'flame-like', Gothic. Perhaps the earliest example of Flamboyant Gothic tracery is to be found in the west rose window of the façade of La Sainte Chapelle, which replaced the earlier Rayonnant window in 1485. The Flamboyant style placed emphasis upon large areas of voids, cut away from the stone mass of the building. It was a dynamic Gothic style full of movement, and Flamboyant tracery features the use of the curved ogee, or four-centred, arch

*Opposite: A study of the polychromy at La Sainte Chapelle, Paris, by J G Crace, 1845. A major programme of restoration took place at La Sainte Chapelle during the 1840s under the supervision of the architect Felix Duban, with Jean Lassus and later, Eugène Viollet-le-Duc. J G Crace, the eminent London interior decorator, was an admirer of Duban and made this drawing of the restored polychromy of the Chapel. Later he visited the châteaux of Blois and Chambord to view their restoration work by Duban.*

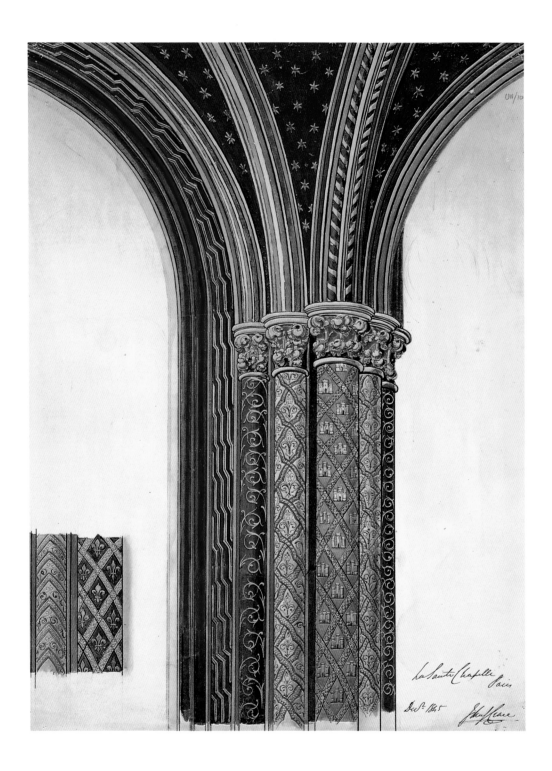

*Vaulting in the Chapel of Henry VII, Westminster Abbey, c1503–9. One of the principal sources for eighteenth-century Gothic Revivalists, this Chapel was built at the east end of Westminster Abbey, probably by the architect Robert Janyns. The richness of the Chapel's decoration, both inside and out, is remarkable. The stone pendants hang down amidst the lacelike tracery of the ceiling, thus stabilizing the transverse arches of the construction.*

*Opposite: Nave vaulting in Westminster Abbey, c1388–1400. Westminster Abbey was built as the great thirteenth-century Gothic church in England with lavish decoration. The bulk of the Abbey was completed in 1272 before the death of Henry III. Its architecture was based upon the new French Rayonnant style, as interpreted by the architect Henry of Reyns. However, the nave was remodelled in the Perpendicular style after 1388 by Henry Yevele.*

*A detail of the tiled floor of the Chapter House at Westminster Abbey, c1253–59. Henry III was a great patron of medieval tile-making who installed tiled floors in his thirteenth-century palace at Clarendon, near Salisbury, as well as in the Chapter House at Westminster. The encaustic technique of tile-making, in which coloured clay was inlaid into a terracotta ground, was used here. This technique was revived in the nineteenth century by ceramicists such as Herbert Minton, who worked with Pugin.*

and swirling teardrop-shaped motifs known as mouchettes.

The early sixteenth-century church of St Maclou in Rouen is an example of the style, which overlapped with the introduction of the Renaissance style in France. The decorative, lacelike quality of Flamboyant tracery made it readily adaptable for use on wooden panelling in furniture and domestic architecture. A number of Flemish paintings of the fifteenth century, studied by Gothic Revivalists such as Pugin, show interiors with carved oak furniture in the Flamboyant Gothic style.

Initially, English Gothic architecture developed along parallel lines to that of the French. Corresponding to Early Gothic in France was Early English Gothic, essentially a style of the thirteenth century, featuring high, narrow, pointed lancet windows and steeply pointed nave arcades. Salisbury Cathedral is often considered to be the classic example of Early English Gothic

architecture, and it inspired a number of architects during the Gothic Revival.

Anticipating, and perhaps inspiring, the development of the more ornate Flamboyant style was Decorated Gothic, a style of the fourteenth century, with its lacelike traceried windows and highly decorative stone vaulting. Decorated Gothic was used especially in the architecture of the west of England during the later Middle Ages. The fourteenth-century Wells Cathedral in Somerset contains spectacular examples of Decorated style tracery and vaulting.

The highly decorative treatment of vaulting on the part of English masons led to a final phase of Gothic architecture, Perpendicular Gothic, which had no real counterpart on the Continent. One exception is the abbey church at Batalha in Portugal, part of which is considered to be Perpendicular in style. It is thought to have been the work of an English or Irish mason and attracted great interest among antiquarians

in the eighteenth century. Perpendicular Gothic received its name from the Gothic Revival architect and scholar Thomas Rickman, who recognized that Late Gothic tracery in England came to resemble a grid of horizontals and verticals at perpendicular angles to one another. Perpendicular vaulting resulted in an almost flat, if highly decorated, ceiling. In the mid-fourteenth-century cloisters of Gloucester Cathedral, an early example of Perpendicular Gothic, an inspired team of masons developed fan vaulting where the colonettes of the walls splayed out at the ceiling into fan-like shapes. This vaulting was much admired and copied during the Gothic Revival.

Undoubtedly the most famous Late Perpendicular structure for the eighteenth-century Gothic Revivalists was the Chapel of Henry VII at Westminster Abbey. It is early sixteenth century in date, and therefore contemporary to French Flamboyant architecture. The stonework of the Chapel roof has remarkable vaults where great pendants of stone are suspended from the transverse arches that hold up the roof. While they create a striking form of architectural decoration, these pendants also have a

structural purpose in stabilizing the vaults of the roof. This aspect of Gothic architecture – namely, the merging of the decorative with the functional – was to appeal greatly to Gothic Revivalists of the nineteenth century. The ceiling of Henry VII's Chapel is an imaginative and skilful development of the Gothic tradition at a time when the revival of classical architecture was well under way in Italy. Many Gothic Revivalists looked to this highly decorative, late phase of English Gothic architecture for inspiration.

Although the Gothic was primarily an ecclesiastical style, Gothic tracery and ornament was adapted for use in grander houses in medieval Europe. However, a limited amount is known about domestic architecture, interiors and furnishings of this time. A few stone houses built before the fourteenth century exist in England and France, but most surviving medieval houses date from the fifteenth and early sixteenth centuries. In northern France and Flanders, the wealth created from trade meant that some merchants could afford to build sophisticated private residences of stone with fine Gothic tracery and decorative details created by the same teams of masons who

*Opposite:* Procession of the
Knights of the Order of
Bath, *by Giovanni Antonio
Canaletto, 1749. This view
of Westminster Abbey shows
the west towers, which were
unfinished at the death of
Henry III in 1272. It was
not until 1743 that
Nicholas Hawksmoor
finally completed them.*

*Details from a timbered
cottage, Coggeshall, Essex
(left), the Monk's House,
Newport, Essex (right)
and Paycocke's House,
Coggeshall, Essex (below),
c1500. A rich tradition of
late medieval domestic
architecture is represented in
the towns of Essex. Many
architectural details were
taken from illuminated
manuscripts and church
sculpture and re-interpreted
in wood for domestic
buildings.*

worked on the cathedrals. One such example
is the Flamboyant Gothic stone townhouse
of the wealthy financier Jacques Coeur in
Bourges, built in the fifteenth century.

A number of the châteaux of the Loire
Valley are largely late medieval in date. An
example is Châteaudun, built in the fifteenth
and early sixteenth centuries for the Counts
of Dunois as a fortified residence to surround
an existing twelfth-century Romanesque
keep. As with so many of the Loire Valley
châteaux, the decoration at Châteaudun
spans the Gothic and Renaissance periods,
with some outstanding Flamboyant-style
Gothic tracery in the fifteenth-century wing,
particularly on the courtyard side of the
building. Because they constitute the largest
and perhaps most beautiful group of late
medieval residences, the châteaux of the
Loire Valley were used as sources for
important domestic architecture during

the nineteenth century in Europe and North
America.

In English fortified domestic residences,
Gothic traceried windows were the decorative focal points, and the oriel window was
an important feature which was to reappear
during the Gothic Revival. In the Middle
Ages, the word 'oriel' could refer either to a
projecting window, often round or octagonal
and cantilevered from the façade of a
building, or an entire small chamber or small
room with an oriel window in it. The
popular Gothic novelist Ann Radcliffe used
the word in the latter sense when describing
the small, private chamber of the ill-fated
Marchioness de Villeroi in *The Mysteries of
Udolpho.*

The early sixteenth-century castle
at Thornbury, the seat of the Duke of
Buckingham, was constructed with complex
clusters of projecting oriel windows, adding

The Dream of Guillaume de Loris *from a Flemish manuscript of c1500. This shows de Loris, one of the two thirteenth-century authors of the courtly love epic,* The Romance of the Rose. *He sits on a carved wooden chair writing beneath a high carved canopy which is backed by a rich, probably Italian, damask. The extraordinary construction of the lectern features a spired tower in two parts on top of a baluster-form support. The latter was a common form of Italian Renaissance table furniture, indicating the late date of the manuscript.*

interest and variety to the façade of the building. Fifteenth-century Crosby Hall in London had a large oriel which functioned like a small hallway. A study of Crosby Hall was published by A C Pugin (the father of A W N Pugin) early in the nineteenth century. Its location made it an attractive candidate for study by Gothic Revivalists.

In manuscripts and paintings of the fifteenth century, especially in Flanders, with its strong tradition of realism in pictorial art, a number of details about Late Gothic interiors can be observed. Floors in good houses were tiled with simple, repeated geometric patterns and limited to a few colours on a terracotta ground. A few early Gothic tiled floors survive, such as the thirteenth century floor made for Clarendon Place, which can be seen in the British Museum. However, humble cottages had dirt or pebble floors, while rushes were sometimes placed over packed earth floors even in better houses.

Carpets were extremely rare owing to their high cost. More luxurious interiors had wooden wall panelling, usually of carved oak in the prevailing Gothic style. In exceptional circumstances, wealthy householders might have sets of tapestries to decorate the walls which would be packed and travel with them from residence to residence. Wall hangings with geometric patterns were more common, and sometimes walls were simply painted with patterns to imitate the effect of textiles. The medieval manor house, Bramall Hall in Cheshire, has remains of this type of wall decoration.

The best medieval furniture was generally made of oak and was of simple joined construction with carved traceried ornament in the Flamboyant style, if Continental, or the Decorated and Perpendicular styles, if English. Peasant furniture such as that depicted in the paintings of Hieronymus Bosch was probably made of soft local

The Table of the Seven Deadly Sins, *by Hieronymus Bosch, c1475. The scenes from the table depict various elements of medieval life and furnishings.*

woods such as pine, ash and beech. Little of this humble furniture has survived. To achieve an effect of richness and some degree of comfort, textiles and cushions were used with joined furniture. For beds, textiles were hung to create canopies, or testers, giving relief from draughts. Textiles were the most costly item of a household and travelled with their owners; they were stored in a locking chest which was often

the best piece of furniture in the house. Some examples of medieval furniture have survived, but artists of the Gothic Revival in the nineteenth century often had to rely on the illustrations of interiors in manuscripts and paintings when designing furniture in the Gothic style.

The survival of the Gothic as an architectural style extended well into the seventeenth century in Britain. It continued

*A tapestry panel from* The Lady and the Unicorn *series, c1485–1500. The six tapestries in this series are among the most famous examples of late medieval decorative art. The series was made for a member of the Le Viste family of Lyon. The theme is the five senses, with this panel illustrating a sixth sense of 'doing right', that was remarked upon by ancient philosophers.*

to be used in contexts where it was already well established, such as in additions to the medieval colleges at Oxford and Cambridge or for smaller churches, especially those in rural areas. A large amount of repair and restoration work was needed continually for existing medieval structures, including the great Gothic cathedrals. There were doubtless a number of workshops all over the country which specialized in the Gothic and which continued to pass on knowledge of the style from master to apprentice.

Examples of the Gothic 'Survival' can be traced into the early years of the

eighteenth century, although they begin to diminish during the later seventeenth century. Evidence that the awareness of the Gothic was lessening can be seen in the number of pattern books and builders' manuals which were published from about 1740 to instruct builders and craftsmen in the use of Gothic ornament. The most famous and influential of these books was Batty Langley's *Ancient Architecture Restored and Improved* of 1741–2, successful enough to be re-issued in 1747 as *Gothick Architecture, Improved by Rules and Proportions*. Langley was a gardener's son whose brother is

*The three scenes of this
Flemish tapestry of c1485
are organized by means of
architectural elements in the
Flamboyant Gothic style.
The ogee arches and use of
cusping were picked up by
Gothic Revivalists in the
eighteenth century.*

remembered as the plagiarizer of the French designer Nicholas Pineau. He published a book of engraved plates with captions aimed at workmen who were involved in restoring medieval architecture. The 'improved' aspect of the title referred to Langley's idea of codifying Gothic architecture into orders, along classical lines. Langley favoured the rich forms of Gothic, particularly the Perpendicular with its ogee arches and foliate ornaments.

Some of the ornamental details published by Batty Langley were creditable, and there can be no doubt that the illustrations in his book were used by builders and carpenters around the country. The direct use of these plates is seen, for example, in the exterior of Pool House, Astley,

Worcestershire, a seventeenth-century house that was 'Gothicized' according to Langley's designs some time in the eighteenth century. Here a favourite Langley motif, the ogee arch sprouting a leaf finial, has been used for windows and gables. The gables along the roofline have traceried windows of quatrefoil form, perhaps inspired by classical rosettes but looking like a garland of clover blossoms strung across the top of the house. The result is charming, if somewhat un-medieval. It was this impurity in Batty Langley's Gothic, with its mixing of classical and Gothic details, which was dismissed with contempt by later Revivalists, beginning with the influential figure of Horace Walpole. However, *Ancient Architecture* filled a need at a time when the Gothic Survival was

coming to an end and the Gothic Revival was just beginning.

Early in the eighteenth century, a small group of castellated buildings began to appear, the work of various architects and antiquarians who were experimenting with medievalism. This meant the construction of one or more asymmetrically placed towers and the use of battlements along the roofline, as these were certainly the two most obvious architectural features of fortified medieval castles.

In most examples where castellation was used early in the eighteenth century, it was where a building was already medieval in date and its owner wished for appropriate architectural 'improvements'. This was the case at the large, late medieval house of Hampton Court in Herefordshire, which was given battlements and turrets in about 1710. An exception to this rule can be seen in Vanbrugh Castle in Blackheath, south London. The English architect John Vanbrugh, better known for his design of the splendidly Baroque Castle Howard, built his own castle in about 1717. It was designed to an asymmetric plan and featured a variety of tower and window shapes and the use of battlements for the square corner towers and for the gateposts.

*'Design for a Doorcase' by Batty Langley, published in* Ancient Architecture, *1741–2. Langley's plates were intended for workmen who had been charged with restoring medieval architecture but had not necessarily had any formal training in medieval styles. The ogee arch sprouting a leaf finial, the flower-like window tracery and the frieze of quatrefoils along the top are all typical of Langley's style.*

*Design for a 'Gothick Window' by Batty Langley, published in* Ancient Architecture, *1741–2.*
*In the eighteenth century Langley's plates were widely used as sources for Gothic Revival architecture.*

One scholar has observed that Vanbrugh may simply have liked the variety of effect possible with medieval architectural forms, rather than wishing to evoke the Middle Ages in association with the structure. In the instance of Vanbrugh Castle, medieval elements of design may have been used simply as an interesting alternative to the more usual classical ones. This suggests that Vanbrugh was anticipating the eighteenth-century aesthetic concept of the Picturesque, which was to become an important ingredient in the early development of the Gothic Revival.

Medievalism was increasingly seen as an interesting alternative to the classical ideas that had dominated European culture and design since the Renaissance. For example, in 1717, the date Vanbrugh began designing his castle, the poet Alexander Pope, whose work is associated with the classically-inspired 'Augustan Age' of English literature, revived the tragic medieval love story of Abélard and Héloise in his poetry.

An even more visible symbol of medieval culture and its importance in English history was the extensive restoration work that took place at Westminster Abbey between about 1713 and 1725, initially supervised by the elderly Sir Christopher Wren. The idea was to finish King Henry III's Abbey as he would have wished it. Wren thought it important to avoid a 'disagreeable mixture' of styles, which he felt no person of taste could approve. Nicholas Hawksmoor, who had assisted both Wren and Vanbrugh, was later responsible for designing the west towers of the Abbey in a manner that befitted the Gothic church. At the same time he was supervising the execution of his design for the quadrangle of All Soul's College, Oxford, also in the Gothic style. Horace Walpole described Hawksmoor's version of the style as 'picturesque scenery, not void of grandeur.'

Thus, by the beginning of the eighteenth century, educated opinion regarding the Gothic had progressed to the point where the style could be found pleasing and appropriate if used within the proper context. The choice of Gothic as the appropriate style of architecture with which to complete or enlarge a medieval building was becoming acceptable, and the Gothic style was soon to emerge from its long hibernation.

*The Rustic Cottage, Stourhead, Wiltshire, after 1779. The cottage can be seen in the famous landscape gardens. In 1806 Gothic details were added to it, as seen here in the ogee arches that support the bench and the frieze of quatrefoils, supposedly designed by the antiquarian John Carter. When walking through the extensive gardens, one could pause at the Rustic Cottage and admire the view.*

**Old** Saint Paul's Cathedral…appears to have been a most stately and venerable pattern of the Gothick style. Milton was educated at St. Paul's School, contiguous to the church; and thus became impressed with an early reverence for the solemnities of the ancient ecclesiastical architecture, its vaults, shrines, iles, pillars and painted glass. *Thomas Wharton,* Milton's Early Poems *(1785)*

*A Gothic Temple, Gothic
Portico, Octangular
Umbrello and Gothic
Temple, published in
Batty Langley's* Ancient
Architecture, *1741–2.
Garden structures provided
both an interesting focal
point in a landscape garden
and an opportunity for
experimentation in domestic
architecture. The use of ogee
arches and pinnacles along
the roofline, as seen in these
designs, was a hallmark of
Langley's garden structures.*

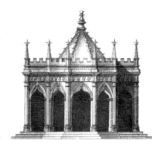

From its tenuous beginnings, the Gothic Revival gained momentum in the first quarter of the eighteenth century. It is difficult to pinpoint any one structure as the first monument of the Revival. Rather, buildings of self-consciously revived medieval style began to emerge in greater numbers during the 1720s and 30s. The landscape gardener and designer Batty Langley spans the Gothic Survival and Revival, and some buildings designed according to the plates he published can be included with the earliest Gothic Revival monuments. However, the intended audience for Langley's pattern book – builders and craftsmen charged with restoring medieval architecture – places it within the lingering twilight of the Gothic Survival.

The earliest distinct group of buildings of the Gothic Revival comprised neither churches nor houses, nor public buildings. It consisted of ornamental structures for landscape gardens, some built of impermanent materials, to add interest to a view or create a vista. Soon afterwards small country houses, or villas, in the revived Gothic began to appear. In the eighteenth century, landscape gardens were a kind of working laboratory for innovations in domestic archi-

tecture. A patron could try out a new style of building by means of a small garden structure before committing himself to the more costly business of building a house in the style. Although almost all of these garden structures have disappeared, they are referred to in literature of the period, including Langley's publications. One example, the Gothic 'Temple' on the grounds of Shotover in Oxfordshire, dates to 1717, the year Vanbrugh was creating his castle. The structure at Shotover was really a glorified garden seat of stone in the form of a giant battlemented gable with a rose window. The Gothic Temple was probably executed by masons working nearby on the medieval monuments of Oxford, and it was designed to add interest to the view across the canal from the house.

In order to understand this earliest group of Gothic Revival buildings, it is useful to examine briefly the English landscape of the eighteenth century and its use of ornamental architecture. It was the leading designer of the Palladian movement, William Kent, who, working during the 1720s and 30s, overthrew the strictures of Baroque garden design. This had been characterized by

*Blaise Castle, Henbury, Bristol, by Robert Milne, 1766. Milne was a well-travelled Scot who settled in London in 1759 and embarked upon a long career as a neo-classical architect. Here he designed a Gothic folly for a picturesque garden.*

highly formal, symmetrical arrangements of planting and sculpture based upon principles worked out by French Baroque designers at grand palaces such as Versailles. For his friend and patron Lord Burlington, Kent created a new type of garden at the latter's highly ornamented Palladian villa at Chiswick. This had formal areas near the house leading into winding avenues, groves of trees, and 'wildernesses' where plantings were informal and natural in appearance. As Horace Walpole was to note, the irregular design of English landscape gardens could be transferred to architecture; asymmetry of design was to become a central principle of the later Gothic Revival.

Certain Baroque painters working in the seventeenth century had promoted a taste for the depiction of wilderness and ancient ruins suggestive of the association between antiquity and the present day. The

serene, allegorical landscapes of Nicholas Poussin and the more emotive scenes of untamed nature painted by Salvator Rosa were both admired during the eighteenth century. Such paintings helped to further the growing taste for the irregularly arranged landscape decorated with ruins from the past in the manner of a picture. Moreover, while classical ruins abounded in Mediterranean Europe, medieval ruins represented the past in Britain, where an informal style of land-scape gardening reached its height. Hence, from its earliest days, the picturesque land-scape had associations with the Gothic style.

William Kent had studied painting and design in Italy for nine years at the outset of the eighteenth century. His architectural and garden designs for his great patron, Lord Burlington, and his circle, were usually laden with references to classical antiquity. However, a small number of Kent's commis-sions were executed in the Gothic style. This interest in the Gothic must have been prompted by Kent's restoration work for several Gothic cathedrals, commissions he received as a result of Lord Burlington's influential connections at Court. At Gloucester Cathedral he designed a Gothic choir screen in 1741 to replace a lost medieval one. This featured the use of ogee arches and finials with sprouting leaves which closely resembled the forms of Batty Langley. A more important commission was the design of a house for the antiquarian Henry Pelham around an existing medieval gatehouse with octagonal turrets. Kent added symmetrical wings with battlementing and recast the windows of the existing structure to be consistent with the new wings. The result was Esher Place in Surrey, begun

*Details of two windows at Stout's Hill, Uley, Gloucestershire, 1743. William Halfpenny, to whom these designs are attributed, was active from the 1720s to the 1750s. He was based in Bristol and worked in the west of England. He published a number of design pattern books, but his name was never as closely linked with the Gothic Revival style as that of his rival, Batty Langley. These window designs bear similarities to those of Langley.*

*Opposite: The Gothic Temple, Painshill, Surrey, c1745. The standard elements of Batty Langley's Gothic style, such as ogee arches, pinnacles and battlements, are seen here. The temple design is actually a simplified version of Plate LVI in Langley's Ancient Architecture, although the builder of this temple is unknown. Walpole criticized the structure, remarking that 'the Goths never built summer houses or temples in a garden.'*

in 1733, which was to inspire Horace Walpole at his later and more famous Gothic Revival house on the Thames, Strawberry Hill.

At Esher, one could say that Kent created a house by adding to a late medieval ruin. He went a step further in the gardens at Rousham in Oxfordshire, where he redesigned an existing mill to impersonate a medieval ruin. The manor house at Rousham was a long, low house of the seventeenth century to which Kent added battlementing on the exterior according to a practice already established by architects like Vanbrugh. Kent's interiors at Rousham were designed in the sumptuous, classically inspired Palladian manner he had created with Lord Burlington, and most of the garden architecture at Rousham was classical in character.

The exceptions to the classicism at Rousham include a delightful building created by Kent in about 1740 known as Cuttle Mill; and, of about the same date, a Gothic 'eyecatcher' on the hill designed in the form of a giant gable with pinnacles. This must have been based upon Kent's observations of Gothic through his restoration work, and quite possibly his observation of the nearby Gothic Temple at Shotover. At Rousham, Kent created medieval 'ruins' to enliven his landscape garden. Cuttle Mill was executed in roughly cut stone with a quatrefoil window and enormous flying buttresses capped by ruinated pinnacles. The effect on the viewer, even today, is highly picturesque and strongly evocative of the vanished medieval past.

*The Gothic Temple (Temple of Liberty), Stowe, Buckinghamshire, begun in 1741. The central part of James Gibb's design, with its large gable and ground-level arcade, is not unlike William Kent's Gothic 'eyecatcher' at Rousham. However, the contrast of two lower side towers with a raised central tower, complete with battlements and pinnacles, imparts great variety to the temple's appearance. The setting is one of the most remarkable landscape gardens of the eighteenth century.*

The final decade of Kent's life, the 1740s, saw the building of a group of garden structures and houses in revived medieval styles by a widening circle of architects, reflecting an increased interest in the Gothic. In 1741 a large Gothic temple in stone was begun in the gardens of Stowe House, Buckinghamshire, which was destined to become the largest neo-classical house in Britain. Kent had been much involved here during the 1730s, although he designed a thoroughly classical landscape garden. The architect of the Gothic Temple at Stowe was James Gibbs, who trained in Rome and is usually remembered as the architect of the highly classically inspired church of St Martin-in-the-Fields in Trafalgar Square, London.

The Gothic Temple at Stowe was placed on the slope of a hill. It had initially been known as the Temple of Liberty, and it reminded the viewer of the medieval origins of British liberties and the signing by King John of the Magna Carta, which limited the power of autocratic rule. The design of Gibbs's temple at Stowe made reference to the Gothic of Kent, with its battlements, crocketted pinnacles and a central tower.

The arcading of the façade, with its single and doubled lancets, bears some fidelity to real Gothic architecture. Most extraordinary was the triangular plan of the building, which in fact derives from the Mannerist architecture of the Elizabethan period. Gibbs's Gothic Temple shares the eclecticism of early Gothic Revival architecture and presents a dramatic and unexpected contrast to its arcadian surroundings, thereby embodying picturesque ideals of landscape design.

One surprisingly early house designed in the Gothic style is Inverary Castle in Scotland by Roger Morris, who, like Kent, is remembered for his architecture in the Palladian manner. Morris began designing the battlemented exterior of Inverary in 1744 for the third Duke of Argyll, who already possessed unexecuted designs for a castle by Vanbrugh. The house is situated beside Loch Fyne, where the land rises dramatically on either shore. Moreover, the new castle was sited beside the ruined late medieval castle of the family, which was later taken down. One eighteenth-century writer, Lord Kames, remarked in 1762 that the choice of the Gothic style was justified in the case of Inverary owing to the wildness of the surrounding landscape. This is an early expression of the idea that the landscape should dictate the appearance of the building sited on it, an idea that the Regency designer Humphrey Repton was to popularize.

In addition to the dramatic setting of Inverary, there were further reasons for this early adoption of the Gothic style for the exterior of the house. Scotland had a very long tradition of fortified castle residences dating back to the Middle Ages. Inverary Castle was designed in this tradition, having

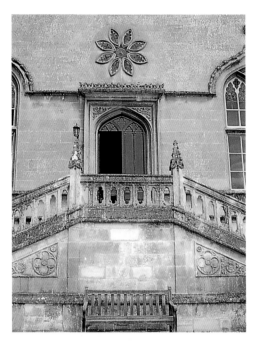

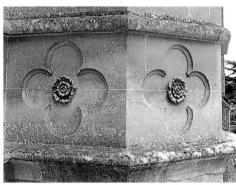

*Lacock Abbey, Wiltshire, details by Sanderson Miller, 1754. Miller redesigned the west façade and Great Hall of the abbey, originally a thirteenth-century convent, for James Ivory Talbot, MP, an enthusiastic antiquary. Miller's motifs, such as the quatrefoils and flower-like window seen here above the entrance, owe much to Batty Langley.*

a massive central block with round turrets at three corners and a large, three-part, square block at the fourth corner facing the loch. In addition to battlements along the roofline, the castle had windows with pointed arches and an entrance with a pointed arch decorated with crockets. Although Morris was an English architect, his work at Inverary signals the way forward for the 'Scottish Baronial' style, an offshoot of the Gothic Revival based upon the regional building traditions of Scotland.

In England in the 1740s, a small but important group of garden buildings followed in the footsteps of Kent's Gothic cottage at Rousham. It is evident from contemporary writings that a number of these Gothic temples and sham ruins were

*The south façade of Arbury Hall, Warwickshire, 1748–70. Sir Roger Newdigate encased his sixteenth-century house within a stone shell, adding battlements, pinnacles, and oriel windows, thus 'Gothicizing' Arbury Hall. The central three-part screen of the south façade is in the Perpendicular style, an example of his archaeologically-based Gothic style. The screen was added in 1770 when the Dining Room was remodelled. The double oriel windows were based upon those which Sanderson Miller used in 1746 for his house, Radway Grange in Warwickshire. Newdigate acted as his own architect, with assistance from the builders William Hiorne, Henry Keene and Henry Couchman.*

*Opposite: The Drawing Room at Arbury Hall, designed in 1762. The plasterwork tracery was taken from Henry VII's Chapel at Westminster Abbey by Newdigate and Keene. The rounded, four-centered shape of the ceiling was probably chosen to display the plasterwork detailing. The most striking feature of the room is the chimneypiece, based upon a thirteenth-century tomb in Westminster Abbey and installed late in 1763.*

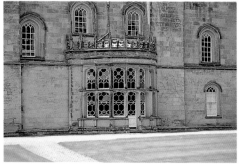

*The east façade of Arbury Hall, probably before 1748. The broad, east bay window has affinities with the designs of Batty Langley and William Halfpenny of the 1740s. It is certainly one of the earliest and least archaeological features of the house, demonstrating how far Newdigate's idea of Gothic was to progress.*

ornaments made of painted canvas and plaster on a wooden frame. These were really like stage sets for the fashionable garden and have long ago vanished owing to the impermanence of their materials. However, a few stone Gothic garden structures of this period have survived.

In 1746 the gentleman-architect Sanderson Miller designed for himself a sham Gothic ruin on a raised site at Edgehill in Radway, Warwickshire, overlooking the location of the first major battle of the English Civil War in 1642. In the following year he added to his castellated tower a rusticated, thatched cottage at its base. Miller's 'ruin' was on the grounds of his own country house, which he began Gothicizing at about the same date. In 1748, Miller added to his monument at Radway, including a fake drawbridge. This left no doubt that he wanted his landscape architecture to evoke the medieval past in vivid fashion. More famous than this garden structure, no doubt due to the wit of Horace Walpole, was Miller's Gothic ruin at Hagley in Worcestershire. It was built in 1748 for his friend Sir George Lyttleton and found much favour with the fashionable world, resulting in further commissions for Miller. Of this

asymmetric cluster of battlemented towers with a ruinated Gothic arcade attached to it, Horace Walpole made the much quoted observation that it had 'the true rust of the Barons' wars.' Walpole approved of the structure because it had the power to evoke the Middle Ages.

Walpole was not always so approving of Miller's Gothic. He disliked the Gothic of Radway Grange, Miller's own country house, probably because of its reliance upon the designs published by Batty Langley. In 1746 Miller had married and been given Radway Grange in Warwickshire, a seventeenth-century manor house, as a home for himself and his bride. He gave the house a new south front in the Gothic style, an appropriate choice as the house occupied the site of a medieval monastic foundation. Miller's new façade featured twin two-storey oriels decorated with tracery and crocketted pinnacles surmounted by pointed gables. Perhaps Miller found it easier to create imaginative monuments of modest scale within a landscape garden than to create a larger medieval style structure such as a country house, with its practical and functional requirements. Furthermore, since Miller's country house architecture consisted of converting structures to the Gothic style, he had to accommodate existing plans and layouts.

Of greater architectural interest are the entrance arch, west façade and Great Hall of Lacock Abbey in Wiltshire, designed by Miller in 1754 for James Ivory Talbot, an MP and antiquary. The abbey had considerable architectural remains, including a cloister from the thirteenth-century medieval convent which had occupied the site until the Reformation. The abbey had been founded by Ela, Countess of Salisbury, who with her husband also founded Salisbury Cathedral; the only possible style for the alterations was, therefore, the Gothic.

The entrance façade on the west range of the building was approached through an ogeed archway of stone capped by giant crocketted pinnacles. The exterior featured two double-lancet windows capped by ogee arches taken directly from Batty Langley's *Ancient Architecture* of 1741. The fact that Miller did not copy details from the existing medieval architecture but instead used the designs of Langley attests to their usefulness to eighteenth-century architects not trained in the Gothic tradition. The wall surface at the upper storey of Miller's façade was left mostly blank, with the exception of an eight-petalled rose in tracery, probably again looking to Langley for inspiration. The interior decoration of the Hall is of interest owing to the use of canopied niches filled with sculpted figures from medieval history, including William Longespee, the husband of the abbey's founder and a witness to the signing of the Magna Carta. The figures were modelled by an Austrian sculptor trained in the Baroque tradition, creating a rather startling stylistic contrast to the medievalisms of the Hall. Four side tables of yew with Gothic details were made for the Hall at the same time, and in Miller's windows were mounted pieces of stained glass surviving from the original Great Hall.

In considering his work overall, Sanderson Miller emerges as a committed and early, if somewhat tentative, architect of the Gothic Revival. Miller did not design a single Gothic Revival house in its entirety, and his work demonstrates a surprisingly hesitant use of the Gothic vocabulary of ornament. However, Miller was working as a talented amateur and had an active period only of about ten years. He struggled with bouts of depression and insanity during the final 20 years of his life, and died in 1780.

If Miller's use of Gothic forms at Radway and Lacock was somewhat restrained, he inspired another gentleman-architect who was to plunge much deeper into the waters of the Gothic Revival. This was Sir Roger Newdigate, whose work at his own house, Arbury Hall in Warwickshire, began in about 1748 in conjunction with Miller. The prominence of independently wealthy, gentleman-amateur architects in the early phase of the Gothic Revival is perfectly natural given that the style was an unusual, if not eccentric, choice for a country house in the middle of the eighteenth century. There were only a few professional builders who were trained in its use. Men like Sanderson Miller, Roger Newdigate and Horace Walpole were to lead the way by (to paraphrase Walpole) pleasing their own tastes and realizing their own visions. Certainly, Newdigate's vision of the Gothic was a scholarly one.

*The Saloon at Arbury Hall, Warwickshire, designed c1765. The plaster vaulting of the Saloon was modelled closely upon the famous Perpendicular Gothic Chapel of Henry VII at Westminster Abbey. In* Mr Gilfil's Love Story, *the novelist George Eliot likened the ceiling to 'petrified lace-work'. The architect, Sir Roger Newdigate, was assisted by Henry Keene, Surveyor to the Fabric of Westminster Abbey.*

*The Dining Room at Arbury Hall, c1770–88. This room was fashioned from the Elizabethan Great Hall of the house and still retains Elizabethan portraits and furnishings. The chimneypiece has an unusual design with two rows of small towers placed on the diagonal. The richly worked and canopied niches are filled with classical figures, perhaps referring to the meeting of Late Gothic with classical forms during the Elizabethan period.*

*A detail of the plasterwork tracery in the Drawing Room ceiling at Arbury Hall, designed in 1762 by Newdigate, assisted by Keene.*

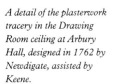

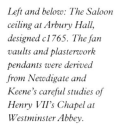

*Left and below: The Saloon ceiling at Arbury Hall, designed c1765. The fan vaults and plasterwork pendants were derived from Newdigate and Keene's careful studies of Henry VII's Chapel at Westminster Abbey.*

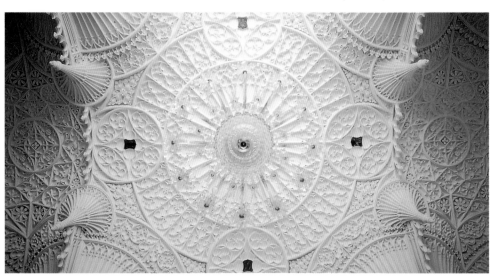

Portrait of Sir Roger
Newdigate *by Arthur
Devis, c1755. The Library,
with its antiquarian
associations, was the first
interior at Arbury Hall
to be Gothicized. Fairly
restrained ogee-arched
bookcases were installed,
together with a tomb-like
chimneypiece; but the
ceiling was not finished
until 1791 when a classical
Roman source was used for
its design.*

The Gothicizing of Arbury Hall proceeded in a slow, painstaking way, reflecting Newdigate's methodical personality. By the mid-1750s he and Miller saw little of one another owing to political differences, but his friendship with Miller had acted as a catalyst for his own experiments in the Gothic style. Moreover, Newdigate and Horace Walpole disagreed in their politics to such an extent that Walpole refused to acknowledge Newdigate's very real contribution to the history of the Gothic Revival in his copious writings. As a result of Walpole's edict of *damnatio memoriae*, Arbury Hall has only recently begun to attract the attention it deserves for its carefully researched Gothic architecture, which reached a degree of fidelity to ancient models equalled only by the later work at Strawberry Hill, Walpole's house.

Arbury Hall had been an Augustinian monastery in the Middle Ages, but it was completely rebuilt in the sixteenth century by a judge in the government of Elizabeth I. When Sir Roger Newdigate, who inherited the house at the age of 14, began to make alterations to Arbury, he was careful to preserve the important Elizabethan portraits and early furniture contained in the house. Gradually he encased the house in a Gothic stone façade, preserving the ancient quadrangular plan. Some of the exterior stone detailing such as the magnificent three-part screen across the south front is of exceptional quality in its modelling, which was based upon the architecture of Westminster Abbey. The screen was in place by 1788, enlarging the Dining Hall of the house.

By 1755, the date at which Walpole was putting the finishing touches on his own Gothic library, Newdigate had turned his attention to the Library at Arbury Hall. The library was often the first room to be remodelled in the Gothic style because of its associations with antiquarian learning and monastic libraries. At Stowe, for example, despite the overwhelming classicism of its architecture, a Gothic library was installed in 1805 to house a fine collection of early medieval manuscripts. The architect was Sir John Soane, who used flattened 'vaulting' taken from the Chapel of Henry VII at Westminster, where he had been involved in restoration work. At Arbury there is a portrait of Newdigate (by the then fashionable portrait painter Arthur Devis) showing him seated in his Gothic library and displaying his own drawing for the room. This ensured that Newdigate claimed recognition for his role as architect.

Sir Roger had attended Westminster School, where he had begun sketching the Abbey. Later, when redesigning his house, Sir Roger turned for assistance to Henry Keene, Surveyor to Westminster Abbey, whose position was one of the most important available to an architect or builder in the eighteenth century. As a result, Keene

knew the Late Gothic Chapel of Henry VII at Westminster extremely well, and its rich, lacelike details and famous pendant vaults began to appear at Arbury.

In 1766 ideas for a new Dining Hall were taking shape (although the room was not finished until ten years later, after Keene's death). The fan-shaped vaults of Henry VII's Chapel were translated by Keene into magnificent fan-like structures that filled the height of the Hall. They were painted in 'stone' colour, along with richly carved and pierced canopies above niches housing, surprisingly, neo-classical sculptures. It is known that Newdigate was an admirer of the work of Wedgwood, but the mixing of classical and Gothic styles may refer to the history of the room itself, as the Banqueting Hall of the Elizabethan house. Portraits and furniture from the Elizabethan period – the transition from late medievalism to the classicism of the Renaissance – were contained in the newly Gothicized Hall.

Even richer was the later sham vaulting of the Saloon on the east side of the house, which was closely based upon the famous stone vaulting at Westminster. This was the architecture described by the nineteenth-century novelist George Eliot as 'petrified lace-work' in *Mr Gilfil's Love Story*. Eliot, or Mary Ann Evans, grew up on the estate and described Arbury Hall under the pseudonym of Cheveral Manor in her series, *Scenes of Clerical Life*, in 1857. Newdigate himself appeared as Sir Christopher Cheveral, the knowledge connoisseur and Gothic enthusiast. Keene actually took plaster casts of ornamental details at Westminster for use at Arbury, which illustrates how very seriously he and Newdigate researched their Gothic.

*The Drawing Room ceiling at Alscot Park, Warwickshire, c1764. This was the result of the owner, James West's, visit the previous year to Strawberry Hill, where he saw the rich ceiling of the Gallery.*

*A detail of woodwork at Alscot Park, c1760. John Phillips and George Shakespeare were the carpenters who executed the woodwork at Alscot, including this simple ogee arch opening onto the Library.*

*Opposite: A detail of the chimneypiece at Alscot Park, c1750–64. The remodelling at Alscot Park is contemporary with the early work at Arbury Hall, and yet the two represent the opposite ends of the Gothic spectrum. Arbury was based quite literally upon medieval sources; Alscot was an inventive interpretation of the Gothic style, partly based upon Batty Langley's designs, as seen here. Thomas and Edward Woodward were the masons who executed this chimneypiece.*

*Left and right: Two details of the Dining Room at Alscot Park. Ogee arches, tracery and coats of arms mingle with nuts and berries in this highly original carving. The freedom of design is equal to that of Luke Lightfoot at Claydon House, Buckinghamshire, in the 1770s.*

The popular notion that Gothic Revival architecture of the eighteenth century was frivolous in intent and inaccurate in execution can be laid to rest. At Arbury, the architecture was closely based upon the careful study of medieval sources.

Newdigate was not only serious about his use of the Gothic; he made a lifetime's work out of the Gothicizing of his house. In 1781, when Miller was dead and Walpole was an elderly gentleman resting on his laurels, Newdigate was still at work converting the courtyard passage into a proper, Gothic-style cloister. His quest for Gothic at Arbury was to extend over 50 years in all, the house being substantially complete by 1798 with the addition of a richly ornamented bay window on the ground floor. However, minor alterations continued until his death in 1806.

*An engraving after
J H Müntz,* Portrait of
Horace Walpole, *1756. The
greatest of the eighteenth-
century Gothic Revivalists,
Walpole partly designed
and had built the first
completely Gothic house of
the Revival, Strawberry
Hill, beginning in 1750.
Walpole, who is also credited
with the invention of a new
genre of Romantic literature,
the Gothic novel, was a
great collector and promoted
the study of medieval art.
He is depicted here in the
Library, which contained
a sizeable collection of
antiquarian books.*

While Arbury was undergoing a programme of Gothicization, Newdigate and
Keene, working together, were to spread
the vaults and tracery of Henry VII's Chapel
to the interiors of University College Hall,
Oxford (where Newdigate had been an
undergraduate), and 18 Arlington Street,
London, in the 1760s. The latter was the
townhouse of the Countess of Pomfret,
Newdigate's relation by marriage. Pomfret
Castle, as it was otherwise known, had a
Gothic exterior that was very probably
designed by Sanderson Miller. It must
have looked quite remarkable in the
London of the 1760s, then in the throes of
the neo-classicism being promoted by the
young Scottish architect Robert Adam.
Unfortunately it was demolished early in
this century.

Sanderson Miller, by virtue of the early
date of his Gothic enthusiasms, and Sir
Roger Newdigate, because of the longevity
and seriousness of his Gothic vision, both
deserve a place in the history of the early
Gothic Revival. However, the figure who
dominated the Revival in the eighteenth
century was Horace Walpole. A small,
frail man of literary tastes, Walpole was
the unlikely son of the robust Sir Robert
Walpole, the most powerful British Prime
Minister of the eighteenth century. Horace
Walpole grew up in a palatial residence
designed by William Kent. He quickly
tired of the political scene, instead cultivating
an international circle of friends and
acquaintances with whom he carried on a
voluminous correspondence. His letters,
unquestionably written with posterity in
mind, have been published and read since
the nineteenth century and are among the
classics of English writing.

Walpole has further claims to literary
fame. In 1764 he wrote what was to become
the first Gothic novel, *The Castle of Otranto*,
which inspired subsequent writers in this
genre, including the great Sir Walter Scott.
Scott once said of Walpole, in a preface to
a nineteenth-century edition of *Otranto*,
'He brings with him the torch of genius, to
illuminate the ruins through which he loves
to wander.' In addition to his successful
Gothic novel, Walpole published a four-
volume history of art, *Anecdotes of Painting*,
in 1761–71, which is still used today. Finally,
Walpole wrote and published through his
own press a *Description of Strawberry Hill*
(1774 and 1784), in which the architecture,
interiors  and collections of his Gothic
Revival house were recorded and explained.

*An illustration from*
The Castle of Otranto, *by Horace Walpole, published by Cooper and Graham in 1796. Walpole's book (first published in 1765) is widely recognized as the first example of the Gothic novel. He used his recently remodelled Gothic house, Strawberry Hill, as the setting for some of the important scenes in the book. Here Matilda sets free the hero of the book, Theodore, whom her father has wrongly imprisoned.*

*The upper staircase by Richard Bentley and Horace Walpole at Strawberry Hill, Twickenham, 1753–4. Originally the walls were a neutral stone colour, with painted Late Gothic tracery derived from an antiquarian book owned by Walpole that illustrated Prince Arthur's tomb in Worcester Cathedral. Bentley also used Continental sources, seen in the pierced balustrading, with its flower-like forms and cusped mouchettes. Walpole described the staircase as 'the most particular and chief beauty of the castle' in 1753, when it was being decorated.*

*A doorcase by Thomas Pitt in the Gallery at Strawberry Hill, c1763. The richly detailed canopies and 'vaulting' of the ceiling, derived from Westminster Abbey, were executed in papier mâché, a substance that was gaining in popularity over plasterwork as it was less time-consuming and inconvenient to install. Thomas Pitt, later Lord Camelford, designed the curious Gothic trelliswork of this doorcase, which led into Walpole's little Cabinet, a room with 'all the air of a Catholic chapel'.*

'My house is but a sketch by beginners', wrote Walpole modestly of the work at Strawberry Hill. There can be not the slightest doubt, however, that Walpole was anxious to ensure that his achievements were recognized.

In 1747 Walpole leased a small house in Twickenham on the Thames. For the wealthy son of a famous prime minister, it was a modest house albeit in an excellent location, set in the thick of fashionable villas and rural retreats and overlooking the Thames traffic. In 1749 Walpole liked his house well enough to buy it, with a mind to enlarging it, and by 1750 he had decided on the Gothic style for the rebuilding. In this he was influenced by William Kent. Walpole had grown up in a house designed by Kent, and he knew and admired Kent's part-

medieval Esher Place, which was just down the river from Strawberry Hill. Additionally, Walpole was known to favour the irregularity and asymmetry Kent had introduced into garden design. It is clear from Walpole's letters that, from the first, he had intended his house to be asymmetric in plan, a novel feature not used by either Miller or Newdigate, and one destined to become central to Gothic Revival architecture of the nineteenth century. Not every observer was pleased with the results of Walpole's choice of house, however. As one society matron remarked when she saw it, 'Jesus God, what a house.'

Walpole had a clear and original vision of what he wanted to achieve in architectural terms, but he needed practical assistance in

*An illustration of the Gallery, published in Walpole's* Description of Strawberry Hill, *1784. With the creation of this large and imposing room, designed by John Chute and Thomas Pitt in 1760–3, Walpole remarked 'We have dropped all humility in our style'.*

*An illustration of the Library, published in Walpole's* Description. *Here, in one of the most important early interiors (designed in 1753–4), Walpole and Chute again turned to illustrations in antiquarian books for inspiration. They adapted designs from the old Gothic St Paul's Cathedral for bookcases, while the chimneypiece was derived from prints of two medieval tombs. The Library's design was therefore inspired by the volumes it contained.*

The Library, Strawberry Hill, Twickenham, by John Chute and Horace Walpole, 1753–4. Walpole used the theme of heraldry, incorporating a great number of coats of arms of his ancestors, both real and imaginary.

Opposite: The Gallery at Strawberry Hill, by Thomas Pitt and John Chute, 1760–3. The Gallery signalled the development of Walpole's interest in copying real medieval monuments rather than relying upon printed sources, as he had previously done. In this case the source was Henry VII's Chapel at Westminster Abbey.

The chimneypiece in the Great Parlour at Strawberry Hill, by Richard Bentley, 1753–4. The charming but unreliable Bentley occupied a place in Walpole's 'Committee of Taste' for about ten years before the two men quarrelled and separated. Bentley often relied upon lacelike tracery and Flamboyant Gothic elements for his designs. In Carter's watercolours of the Strawberry Hill interiors, done in 1788, the chimneypiece is illustrated with no saints in the niches but with pots displayed amidst the pinnacles on the top.

realizing that vision. He turned to his friend of long standing, John Chute, who was, like himself, a gentleman architect. Chute had inherited a rambling late medieval house of great charm called The Vyne in Hampshire, to which he was to make alterations in the classical and Gothic styles. Chute's architectural drawings may have been amateurish in execution, but they had the merit of setting forth the ideas for the initial phase of Strawberry Hill beginning in 1750, until Walpole turned to professional architects for assistance. The exterior of Strawberry Hill was designed by Walpole and Chute with battlements and crocketted pinnacles along the roofline. Quatrefoil windows in the manner of Batty Langley were used along the upper storey of the façade, while the lower two stories had double-pointed windows with dripstone mouldings and a central, projecting, polygonal bay. It is

typical of Walpole that, although he was later to denounce Langley's 'bastard Gothic', he owned a copy of Ancient Architecture and used it as a source.

It is the interiors, rather than merely the exterior of the house, that make Strawberry Hill such a landmark in the Gothic Revival. Unlike any other house of the middle of the eighteenth century, Strawberry Hill was entirely designed and remodelled in the Gothic style, inside and out. While the early rooms such as the Great Parlour appear to be somewhat tentative in their Gothic dress, the interiors as a whole represented a watershed in eighteenth-century taste. As the first complete house of the Gothic Revival, Strawberry Hill made the style a serious option for fashionable furnishings and interior decoration. Thomas Chippendale's book, The Gentleman and Cabinet-Maker's Director, published in 1754, was the first pattern book devoted to furniture design, and included designs in the Gothic style, very likely due to Walpole's influence.

A lively mind was called upon for assistance with the interiors. This was in the person of Richard Bentley, the son of a well-known academic, who was clever and gifted but undisciplined. Walpole eventually despaired of him. Bentley designed a series of illustrations full of charm for Walpole's publication of the poems of Thomas Gray in 1753. Gray, who had a genuine appreciation of medieval architecture, had accompanied Walpole on his Grand Tour of the Continent in 1739. The two had admired Gothic cathedrals and shared the sublime experience of a thunderstorm while crossing the Alps. The success of Bentley's illustrations led Walpole to co-opt him onto the 'Committee of Taste', which already included Walpole and Chute, for the designing of Strawberry Hill. Ultimately, Bentley's designs were to prove too fanciful for Walpole's intentions, but his imprint can be seen in the early interiors.

Watercolours by John Carter, executed in 1788, record the appearance of the principal Strawberry Hill interiors. This was another of Walpole's achievements; the commission represents the first systematic record of house interiors to be made, and it demonstrates Walpole's great interest in collections and furnishings as an aspect of design. The Great Parlour had a papier mâché pendant frieze in the manner of Batty Langley around the room, and the focus of interest was the highly crocketted and pinnacled chimneypiece by Bentley. Its shape was loosely based upon Gothic tomb design, but it was a product of Bentley's fertile imagination with its lacelike forms.

The walls of the Parlour were decorated in textured wallpaper to imitate stucco, and woven rush matting was used on the floor, perhaps because of its associations with medieval banqueting halls. Walpole wanted some appropriately Gothic furniture for this room, and after a detailed correspondence with Bentley managed to elicit from him designs for a set of chairs. (This was in 1754, when Bentley was in Jersey to escape his creditors.) The backs, according to Walpole's instructions, were designed to resemble traceried stained glass windows from a Gothic cathedral.

Bentley's chairs, made by the London cabinet-maker William Hallett, were of great originality, being closer to medieval Gothic in their tracery than the designs published by Thomas Chippendale. In addition, and unlike Chippendale, Walpole intended that the finish of the chairs, in ebonized beech, should follow medieval precedent. He had seen ebony chairs at Esher and believed them to be of Tudor date, having 'the true black blood', as he put it. The ebony furniture Walpole used as a source was, in fact, of seventeenth-century date. However, Walpole believed it to be medieval and wanted furniture as authentically Gothic as possible for Strawberry Hill. To complement these chairs, ebonized frames were also supplied by Hallett in 1755. A large side table of the true black blood was supplied the following year. This furniture was sold from Strawberry Hill after Walpole's death and purchased by a member of the Chute family for The Vyne.

The Library of Strawberry Hill, finished in 1754, was perhaps the most important early interior in the house. As Strawberry

*A chair designed by Richard Bentley and Horace Walpole, 1754, from the Great Parlour at Strawberry Hill, Twickenham. Bentley's distinctive, lacelike traceried forms can be seen in the back of this beech chair, one of a set designed for the Great Parlour. Walpole corresponded with Bentley late in 1754, specifying a black finish for the chairs, as he believed that ebony furniture was used in the Middle Ages. William Hallett of London made this and other Gothic furniture for Walpole.*

*A mahogany chair, possibly after the designs of Robert Manwaring, c1770. Like the chairs at Strawberry Hill, the back was modelled after a Gothic window. However, the design is less original than that of Bentley, featuring narrow, repeated lancets. Manwaring published two pattern books in 1765 containing designs for chairs in the Gothic style. J H Müntz, a member of the Strawberry Hill circle, contributed plates to Manwaring's books.*

Hill progressed, Walpole demanded from his Committee designs that were increasingly closely modelled upon the illustrations of Gothic architecture and monuments in his own collection of books. As the emphasis was directed more and more towards the faithful use of medieval sources for designs, the sober John Chute emerged as the favoured designer over the imaginative Richard Bentley. The latter's design of 1753 for the Library bookcases, with pleasingly eccentric arches with double pinnacles, was politely rejected in favour of Chute's quite literal adaptation of an antiquarian print by Wencelaus Hollar of the choir of the Gothic St Paul's Cathedral in London, which had perished in the Great Fire of 1666. The chimneypiece was modelled upon a print of

a tomb, and panels of late medieval stained glass were inserted into the window panes, as they had been in the Great Parlour. The painted ceiling was designed by Walpole and Bentley to incorporate coats of arms of Walpole's ancestors, real and imaginary. A preoccupation with genealogy and the decorative use of heraldry were to become an aspect of the Gothic Revival. As Sir Walter Scott was to observe, Walpole's respect for birth and rank predisposed him towards the Gothic style.

Walpole's interest in the appropriate furnishing of his Gothic interiors gathered pace in the second phase of Strawberry Hill, from about 1758 to 1763. Two principal interiors of this second phase of Gothic were the Holbein Chamber and the Gallery.

The Holbein Chamber had a suite of ebony furniture bought by Walpole at auction. This was a significant step away from having designs produced 'in the manner of' and towards furnishing with antiques – an unusual, if not eccentric, practice in the middle of the eighteenth century.

The Holbein Chamber took its name from the copies of Holbein's paintings made by George Vertue that were housed within it. Other antiquarian objects of appropriate date or with Tudor associations were contained within the room, which functioned as a combination guest bedroom and museum. The bed was screened by a magnificent piece of carved and pierced traceried woodwork based upon a design by Bentley and incorporating inspiration from the late Gothic choir screen of Rouen Cathedral. The fact that a French model should be used indicates the broadening of Walpole's Gothic vision. The poet Gray remarked

that he considered the Holbein Chamber to be the best thing Walpole had yet done. However, greater triumphs were to come.

In 1760 the Gallery at Strawberry Hill was begun and it was finished three years later. Walpole wrote to a friend, 'We have dropped all humility in our style', describing the Gallery as 'richer than the roof of Paradise.' Its scale was dramatically increased over the smaller, more intimate rooms of the 1750s. Here the stone-coloured ceiling contrasted with red silk hung on the walls. The ceiling had papier mâché sham vaults copied directly from the pendant vaulting of Henry VII's Chapel at Westminster Abbey, the same source that Newdigate and Keene were then studying for Arbury Hall. This was a turning point for Walpole, from reliance on prints of Gothic architecture to first-hand experience of medieval buildings as sources.

Walpole must have been especially proud of the design of his gallery. Shortly

*The doorcase in Lady Waldegrave's Drawing Room, c1860–3, at Strawberry Hill. The Countess Waldegrave loved the eighteenth-century Gothic architecture of Strawberry Hill, which her husband had purchased after Walpole's death. However, as a leading political hostess, she needed large rooms for entertaining. She set about designing a new Gothic wing in about 1860, attempting to create interiors that were sympathetic to the eighteenth-century house. The round pediment of this doorcase is a classical form and has no precedent in Walpole's work.*

after it was finished, he used it as the setting for several scenes in his novel, *The Castle of Otranto*, including the scene where the servants Diego and Jaquez witness the supernatural appearance of a giant foot clad in armour. The young hero of the book, Theodore, proves his bravery by volunteering to return to the Gallery to investigate. In the preface to the first edition of the novel, owing to his nervousness at revealing himself to be the author, Walpole claimed the manuscript had been discovered 'in the library of an ancient Catholic family in the North of England.' He mischievously suggested that the architecture was so vividly described in the novel that 'The scene is undoubtedly laid in some real castle…the author had some certain building in his eye.' This building was, of course, Strawberry Hill.

Off the Gallery was the Tribune, completed a year later. It was an ornate little room of unusual quatrefoil shape that had

'all the air of a Catholic chapel', according to Walpole. The ribbed and vaulted roof was lit with a star in yellow stained glass, which he claimed was based upon the Chapter House of York Minster. In fact, Chute had adapted tracery from the great west window of York. The poet Gray described the Tribune as 'all Gothicism and gold and crimson'. It was a rich little room in the new Gothic manner of Strawberry Hill of the 1760s, and its intimacy of scale created an architectural complement to the grand scale of the Gallery.

The character of the Strawberry Hill Committee of Taste changed after the departure of Richard Bentley in 1759. Thomas Pitt, another talented amateur with the archeological leanings of Newdigate, had replaced the disgraced Bentley on the Committee and assisted with the Gallery. One of the more interesting professional designers associated with the Strawberry Hill circle was a native of Alsace named Johann

*Brizlee Tower at Hulne Park, Northumberland, c1781. The ground storey of this tower is derived from the garden 'porticoes and temples' designed by Batty Langley in 1741–2. However, the tower itself may owe something to Sanderson Miller's commemorative towers at Radway and Hagley of the 1740s. Robert Adam, to whom the design is attributed, worked nearby at Alnwick Castle in the Gothic style.*

*Culloden Tower at Richmond, Yorkshire, c1775. The Battle of Culloden and the final defeat of the Stuart cause captured the public imagination in the eighteenth century, and, curiously, came to be associated with the Gothic style. This may have been due to the medieval origins of the Stuart dynasty.*

Heinrich Müntz. He travelled widely in his career, arriving in England in 1755 where he was introduced to Walpole by Bentley. Müntz had studied Moorish architecture in Spain in the 1740s and Egyptian and Roman antiquities early in the 1750s. In 1759 he designed his greatest work in England, an ornamental Gothic 'Cathedral' for Kew Gardens which has long since disappeared, being made of painted plaster and wood. Müntz's drawing for it in the Metropolitan Museum of Art in New York reveals an extremely competent essay in Flamboyant Gothic with twin towers, a pierced parapet, pinnacles, and niches for sculpture. The 'Cathedral' at Kew was one in a series of monuments representing the styles of architecture conceived of by the Crown architect, William Chambers.

After this, the two leading professional architects of the day, Robert Adam and James Wyatt, prepared Gothic designs for Strawberry Hill. Wyatt designed offices for Walpole in 1790, while Adam designed the ceiling and chimneypiece of the Round Room off the Gallery and a rather splendid traceried settee in about 1765. Although he is known for his neo-classical architecture, Adam's interest in medieval architecture was more than superficial. He rebuilt and designed a group of medieval castles in Scotland and the North of England, including Alnwick in Northumberland, seat of the Dukes of Northumberland. Most of these had dramatic, elevated sites and featured battlemented towers with fortified walls and ramparts. For the Chapel at Alnwick, in the 1770s, Adam designed a set of traceried chairs based upon the medieval Coronation Chair of Edward II in Westminster Abbey. This was one of the few authentic pieces of medieval furniture to be seen and recognized as such in the eighteenth century. It is understandable that Adam, who did so much to promote the application of scholarship to classicism, should take the same approach towards designing in the Gothic style.

Walpole frequently used the word 'Catholic' in association with the Gothic style, and it is important to bear in mind the restricted position of Roman Catholics in the eighteenth century. Catholics were officially not allowed to vote or to own property, although in practice this was rarely enforced. Catholic Mass was quietly observed in private chapels, usually belonging to country houses. The Gothic style in the eighteenth century had strong associations with medieval Catholicism which were to be furthered in the nineteenth century by the writings of A W N Pugin. Catholic patrons were to occupy a prominent position in the Gothic Revival.

*A detail of star vaulting (left) and a doorcase (right) at Charleville Forest, Co. Offaly, Ireland, begun c1800. The house was designed by Francis Johnston. The first Earl of Charleville, who commissioned it, was an admirer of Strawberry Hill and actually purchased a chair designed by Bentley for the Great Parlour from the sale following Walpole's death. The Gallery ceiling at Charleville was modelled after the fans and pendants of the Strawberry Gallery, while this star vault may have been inspired by that of Walpole's Cabinet off the Gallery.*

*Opposite: The Library at Milton Manor, Oxfordshire, designed in 1764. Milton's new owner was a convert to Catholicism and a supporter of Bonnie Prince Charlie. The quatrefoils, ogee arches and pendant frieze all reveal that the architect, Stephen Wright, owed a debt to Batty Langley.*

In Oxfordshire there survives a small group of houses of recusant families who refused to give up their Catholic faith at the time of the Reformation. In recusant houses the Gothic style was adopted for its associations with the medieval Church. This was the case at Stonor Park, a rare example of a country house of medieval origin owned by the same family since the Middle Ages. In about 1759 a Gothic chapel was built and the Great Hall of the late medieval house was remodelled in the Gothic style, with fanciful designs of tracery coloured in red and blue and decorated with heraldic themes. Very near to Stonor Park was the Gothic Revival Chapel at Mapledurham, a recusant house with a long medieval history. Both the Stonor and Mapledurham chapels feature wooden ribbed 'vaulting' and tracery with tall pointed lancets. For Stonor, a suite of Gothic seat furniture with pierced backs with flower-like rosettes was made by a local craftsman. This

work came shortly after Walpole's first phase of work at Strawberry Hill, which may have inspired the Gothic alterations at Stonor. However, the latter work was unarcheological, if picturesque, in character and distinct from the scholarly approach of antiquarians like Walpole and Newdigate, who copied medieval architecture.

Of a different character again was the delightful Library at Milton Manor, Oxfordshire, a seventeenth-century house with extensive alterations made in the eighteenth century for a new owner, the prosperous lace-maker and fervent convert to Catholicism, Bryant Barrett, who had been a supporter of Bonnie Prince Charlie and the Stuart cause. In 1764 the architect Stephen Wright designed for him the Gothic Library at Milton, with woodwork carved by a Londoner, Richard Lawrence. The ogee-arched bookcases and windows topped by leaf finials and the pendant frieze around the

room strongly suggest that Batty Langley's plates were used as the basis of the design. A suite of mahogany chairs with backs designed like triple lancets remains in the Library, although these may be of later date than the fittings of the room.

For reasons other than religion, a Gothic room was installed at Claydon House, Buckinghamshire, during the 1770s. The house is an example of Late Palladianism with interiors featuring the full range of styles current in the mid-eighteenth century, from the Palladian to the Chinese. All have superb woodwork by Luke Lightfoot of London, who must rank as one of the greatest and most eccentric talents among eighteenth-century carvers. On the first floor of the house, next door to its remarkable Chinese Room with its carved alcove for taking tea, was the Gothic Room. While overall the room owes a debt to Batty Langley, some of the details found here are distinctly Islamic in character. Islamic designs were sometimes mixed with the Gothic, as Christopher Wren had suggested an Islamic origin for the pointed arch in his writings in the seventeenth century. At Claydon, the Gothic style was not used for its antiquarian or religious associations, nor was it used to legitimize a family pedigree. It was used, rather, for its novelty and variety within the sequence of interiors, forming an interesting contrast to the Chinese designs next door. This places the varied Claydon interiors of the 1770s squarely within the aesthetic framework of the Picturesque.

Richard Payne Knight was the aesthete and designer who promoted the idea of contrasting art historical styles as a means of expressing the Picturesque. He was another in a long line of gentleman amateur-architects who was a Fellow of the Society of Antiquaries and a Dilettante. His family had recently acquired wealth through his father's iron foundry in Shropshire, and Payne Knight wished to build a family seat on a dramatic site high above a rocky gorge. The 1770s, when Claydon was in progress, saw him dividing his time between travel on the Continent, an essential ingredient in every gentleman's education, and designing his seat, Downton Castle. The castle was almost complete by 1778.

Payne Knight wanted to evoke the appearance of a massive, ancient castle rather than literally reproducing one. Using an irregular plan, he designed a severe block between two massive battlemented towers that resembled a Norman keep. Few windows appeared in the masonry walls of the entrance façade, although the south front, facing the gardens, had traceried windows. (The oriels were a later addition.) The interiors of the castle were in the style of Adam's neoclassicism, a stylistic incongruity that Adam himself used, as Payne Knight and Adam believed that battlements had been used in classical times. Payne Knight, author of *An Analytical Enquiry into the Principles of Taste* (1805), found the contrast of styles to be the best means of expressing picturesque taste.

This had already been seen in the architecture of the Irish country house Castle Ward in County Down, begun in 1762 and thought to be the work of an architect from Bristol. Here the entrance façade was in a classical Palladian style, while the garden façade was Gothic. Walpole had contrasted the classical with the Gothic, remarking that

*A view of Shankhill Castle, Co. Kilkenny, Ireland, by George Miller, 1814. The Castle was designed c1800 by the architect William Robertson, making it a contemporary to that at Charleville.*

*A print of the gate at Heywood, Co. Laois, Ireland, by Frederick William Trench, 1818. The bold towers of the gateway would have created a picturesque effect in the surrounding landscape, suggesting the fortified gateways of walled medieval cities.*

*The Gate Lodge,
Glin Castle, Co. Limerick,
Ireland, c1815. The present
Glin Castle was built late in
the eighteenth century and
Gothicized shortly after-
wards by the 25th Knight
of Glin, who also had this
Gate Lodge built. The round
turrets and battlements
recall the destruction of the
medieval Castle in a battle
of 1600.*

*Charleville Forest,
Co. Offaly, Ireland, by
Francis Johnston. Shortly
before 1800 Johnston
designed this asymmetric,
battlemented seat for the
First Earl of Charleville. It
was to become Johnston's
most famous work, perhaps
because of its dramatic,
150-foot tower housing the
star-vaulted 'Boudoir'.*

*Opposite: The Sitting Room
at Castle Ward, Co. Down,
Northern Ireland, c1760–3.
The details of the
extraordinary ceiling are
derived from Henry VII's
Chapel at Westminster
Abbey. However, the
polygonal shapes of the
'vaults' are highly original,
and without a precedent.*

'the Grecian is only proper for magnificent and public buildings'; hence the classical style of the public entrance front at Castle Ward, while Gothic is 'venerable and picturesque', and therefore appropriate for a more private garden façade. Here was the same variety of style seen in the interiors of Claydon applied to the exterior of the house. Castle Ward boasts a most extraordinary sitting room with a ceiling derived from Henry VII's Chapel at Westminster Abbey, only each pendant was executed as polygonal in shape. The result was likened by one witty observer to sitting beneath the udders of a cow. The contrast of styles at Castle Ward was in part due to the disagreement of husband and wife, for while Lady Anne Ward preferred the Gothic, her husband preferred the Palladian.

In addition to promoting a taste for the mixing of styles, Richard Payne Knight, in his concept of the Picturesque, also expressed an inclination for rugged landscapes and dramatic sites, a taste reflected in contemporary literature. The Gothic novelist Ann Radcliffe, who began publishing in the 1790s, almost always used wild forests or rugged mountain ranges on the Continent as the settings for her novels. Her heroines had to confront the supernatural in a variety of ruined and haunted medieval castles and abbeys. The drama and power of Mrs Radcliffe's settings was reflected in a group of picturesque castles placed dramatically on elevated sites succeeding Payne Knight's Downton Castle in the early nineteenth century.

As the taste for the Picturesque developed during the eighteenth century, the search for effects of surprise, variety and novelty intensified, and a reaction against the rational rules of the classical tradition resulted in a dramatic shift in mood towards a phenomenon known as Romanticism. A new aesthetic category, the Sublime, had first been defined by Edmund Burke in 1757 in his *Philosophical Enquiry into the Origin of our Ideas on the Sublime and the Beautiful*. Sublime architecture was designed to evoke strong feelings of awe and wonder on the part of the spectator and it therefore anticipated Romanticism.

*Windsor Castle by Moonlight, by Henry Pether, 1850. In this Romantic view, Windsor Castle takes on a fairy-tale quality as its irregular silhouette and varied towers are seen against the skyline.*

Emily gazed with melancholy awe upon the castle … for, though it was now lighted up by the setting sun, the gothic greatness of its features, and its mouldering walls of dark grey stone, rendered it a gloomy and sublime object … it seemed to stand the sovereign of the scene, and to frown defiance on all who dared to invade its solitary reign. *Ann Radcliffe,* The Mysteries of Udolpho *(1794)*

*A watercolour by J W M Turner, 1794, showing Llanthony Abbey, Wales. The painting, of which there are several versions, suggests the brooding, even potentially violent, quality of an artist such as Salvator Rosa, who was much admired in the eighteenth century. The dark colouring and looming mountain behind the abbey place this image within the early Romantic Movement, which readily assimilated the Gothic Revival.*

By 1800 the grip of the classical tradition on European culture had loosened to a great extent. The Romantic Movement, with its emphasis upon the individual and the cult of human genius, was under way. While Sir Roger Newdigate's approach to designing Arbury Hall typifies the rational attitude of the eighteenth-century man of taste, Horace Walpole, who observed that one needed passion to appreciate the Gothic, anticipated better the Romanticism of the early nineteenth century, with its play upon emotions rather than reason. It is to the architect James Wyatt, whose taste and 'genius' were praised by Walpole, that we return in order to pick up the story of the Gothic style during the Romantic period.

Wyatt had the largest practice of any eighteenth-century architect, and his early training had grounded him thoroughly in the classical tradition. The son of a builder from Staffordshire, he spent six years in all studying in Italy: two in Venice followed by four years in Rome. This was during the period 1762 to 1768, when Robert Adam was rising to fame in Britain. Upon his return to London, Wyatt embarked upon a very successful career, beginning with the design of the Pantheon on Oxford Road in 1772. This was the first major public building in the neo-classical style in Britain, and it stunned contemporaries with its vast scale and richness of ornament, two features that were to distinguish Wyatt's later Gothic

*A print after the portrait of James Wyatt by W Beechy. The greatest Gothic Revival architect of his generation, Wyatt was responsible for Fonthill Abbey and the remodelling of Windsor Castle in the Gothic style for George III. These buildings captured the imagination of the public across Europe.*

buildings. Certainly with regard to vastness, Wyatt's work reflects the aesthetic category of 'the Sublime', as defined by the philosopher Edmund Burke in the middle of the eighteenth century. George III had greatly admired the Pantheon, which led to important professional appointments for Wyatt. In 1776, when still a young man, he succeeded Henry Keene as Surveyor to Westminster Abbey, the major source of inspiration for Gothic Revivalists of the day. Twenty years later, at the height of his career, Wyatt was appointed Surveyor General to the Crown. This confirmed his position as the leading professional architect of his generation.

Despite the neo-classical commissions that he undertook throughout his career, Wyatt's fame rests upon his work in the Gothic style, for which he seems to have had a special sympathy. His work in the medieval manner included the building of a number of 'castles' and the remodelling of existing houses with medieval associations such as Cassiobury in Hertfordshire, which the German traveller and writer Prince Pückler-Muskau visited in 1826 and described as 'modern gothic, and magnificently furnished'. By embracing the Gothic style, Wyatt, the Crown Surveyor, ensured its acceptance among the architectural establishment. Indeed, his obituary in the *Gentleman's Magazine* claimed that 'his genius revived in this country the long forgotten beauties of Gothic Architecture.'

The lustre of Wyatt's reputation has been tarnished by certain controversial areas of his career. First, as a result of his government appointments he found himself in charge of a number of ageing, medieval cathedrals which needed repair. His quite ruthless 'restoration' of Salisbury Cathedral in particular, where he cleared away a number of later monuments and architectural features to recreate its medieval appearance earned him the nickname 'Wyatt the Destroyer' from his principal antagonist, the passionate antiquarian John Carter. This unfortunate appellation was later taken up and perpetuated by A W N Pugin. Carter, draughtsman to the Society of Antiquaries of London, wrote an astonishing 212 letters to the *Gentleman's Magazine* during his lifetime, vigorously denouncing Wyatt's activities. Carter managed to have Wyatt temporarily blackballed from membership in the Society of Antiquaries in 1797 as a result of his work on the cathedrals.

However, Carter's views were not universally shared. Wyatt's restoration of the Chapel of Henry VII at Westminster, that wellspring of eighteenth-century Gothic,

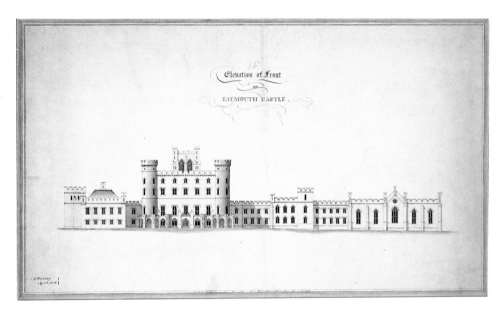

Elevation of Front
or
TAYMOUTH CASTLE.

*Taymouth Castle, Perth-shire, Scotland, depicted by A Murray, 1856. Taymouth is one of the grandest neo-medieval houses in Scotland. Originally a mid-sixteenth-century tower house, the central block with battlements and four corner towers was added in 1810 by the Elliot brothers. The Gothic east range of the house was built by William Atkinson in c1820, giving a pronounced asymmetry of plan. Finally the west wing was remodelled in c1839 by James Gillespie Graham, who was well known for his Gothic Revival houses and who added some splendid Gothic interiors. J G Crace decorated a suite of Gothic interiors for the state visit of Queen Victoria in 1842.*

was considered a success by contemporaries. This was begun in 1809, so Wyatt may have learned from the Salisbury experience. In addition he had as master mason at Westminster the Gothic enthusiast Thomas Gayfere, who had worked for Walpole and took great pains to re-carve accurately stone details in Henry VII's Chapel. Nor was Wyatt's work at Salisbury universally condemned. Prince Pückler-Muskau commented that the cathedral interior had been 'improved by Wyatt's genius. It was an admirable idea to remove the most remark-able old monuments from the walls and obscure corners and to place them in the space between the great double avenues of pillars … Nothing can have a finer effect than these rows of Gothic sarcophagi.'

In addition to the controversy over his philosophy of restoration, Wyatt was hampered by an inability to organize himself or conduct his business in a professional manner. He took on far too many commis-sions at a time and was erratic in supervising his work. He could disappear for months on end, giving himself over to drink and love affairs, while leaving a fuming and exasper-ated patron waiting for him. William Beckford's wrath at Wyatt's conduct has become legendary. Upon hearing of his death in 1813, Beckford remarked that Wyatt had long ago 'sunk from the plane of genius to the mire'. He also said that he spent two years rebuilding the 'villainous' Wyatt's slip-shod work after his death. However, Wyatt's gentlemanly manners were remarked upon by contemporaries, and clearly he possessed great personal charm, upon which he relied too heavily at times. He died suddenly, thrown from an overturned carriage while hurrying from one unfinished job to the next.

Four major commissions in the Gothic style established Wyatt's reputation: Lee Priory in Kent, Fonthill Abbey in Wiltshire,

*An oak armchair, designed by James Wyatt for Windsor Castle, c1805. Here effective use is made of the clustered colonette motif, seen in the legs and back. Other ecclesiastical elements include cusped arches and small quatrefoils set into the frame, like blind tracery in a cathedral.*

the remodelling of Windsor Castle for George III and Ashridge Park in Hertford-shire. Except for Ashridge, this work has almost entirely disappeared and is known principally through contemporary accounts. Lee Priory, the first of these, links Wyatt's Gothic directly to Walpole and Strawberry Hill, where he was to carry out some minor work in 1790.

Walpole had long admired the work of James Wyatt and had recommended him to his friend, the antiquarian collector Thomas Barrett, who owned a modest seventeenth-century house in Kent in need of renovation. In 1783 Barrett decided to adopt the Gothic style for his house, with Wyatt as architect to superintend the transformation. He renamed it Lee Priory as it occupied the site of a medieval monastic foundation. Barrett had apparently considered having the entire house rebuilt in the Grecian style, but in the end he retained this only for his dining room. Walpole was so delighted with the Gothi-cizing of Lee Priory that he later wrote to some friends, advising a visit to the house:

*You will see a child of Strawberry prettier than the parent and so executed and so finished! There is a delicious closet, too, so flattering to me; and a prior's library so antique, and that does so much honour to Mr Wyatt's taste.*

Nor was Walpole alone in his views, for a travel book of the time described Lee Priory as 'one of the happiest examples' of Wyatt's Gothic.

Lee Priory was not a grand country house but a rural villa of modest scale. The gently asymmetric exterior of the building took the form of a battlemented rectangular block with a raised, central section and small octagonal turrets at either side. As Walpole's description implies, the interiors of the house were of greater interest. The 'child of Strawberry' had a cabinet (small room) full of miniatures, like the Holbein Chamber, hence the reason for Walpole being flattered. Upstairs was a 'Strawberry Chamber' with mock fan vaulting and applied motifs of strawberries in plasterwork. It was the Library that received the strongest praise from Walpole, and it is the only room to survive the demolition of the house earlier in this century. Parts of the Library are now installed in the Victoria and Albert Museum in London, where Wyatt's early inspiration in the Gothic can be observed.

The design of the Lee Priory Library must be understood within the context of medieval monastic architecture. Wyatt's scheme suggests the cloistered approach to a monastic library, for the passage to the Library is low-ceilinged, painted in imitation stone colour, and carved in pine to resemble fan vaulting. The famous fan vaulting of the fourteenth-century cloisters at Gloucester Cathedral was a source for the Lee Priory passage, medieval architecture which was much admired in the eighteenth century. In addition, to heighten the effect of a long, low corridor, mirrored panel doors were located at its end, giving the illusion of further recession into the distance. Through an ogee-arched doorcase carved in mock tracery one entered the high-ceilinged Library of Lee Priory. The walls of the Library were covered with bookcases carved with trefoil friezes along their tops. Dividing the cases into bays were clustered colonettes in the manner of the nave of a Gothic cathedral. The bookcases were stone colour, but are now coloured in deep blue and red that may have been added later, when the architect George Gilbert Scott worked on the house. Walpole pronounced the Library to be 'perfect', having 'all the air of an abbot's study excepting that it discovers more taste.'

The exterior of Lee Priory had an octagonal tower above the Library, emphasizing the importance of this room among the Gothic interiors. Octagonal towers had not yet been established in the vocabulary of the Gothic Revival, although they were to become widely used after Fonthill Abbey. Wyatt's tower at Lee Priory must have been inspired by one of two famous medieval

examples. The first was the famous octagonal Lantern of Ely Cathedral, a study of which had been published in 1771 by the antiquarian James Bentham. The Lantern at Ely was a structure of great interest to eighteenth-century scholars.

A more exciting discovery was coming to light at exactly the time that Wyatt began work at Lee Priory. In 1783 the Irish antiquarian Colonel William Conyngham, the patron of Wyatt at Slane Castle, County Meath, visited Batalha Abbey in Portugal, a structure of interest to a British audience because parts of the abbey were supposedly the work of an English mason in the fifteenth century. Conyngham was sufficiently inspired by his visit to engage the Irish architect James Murphy in 1788 to go to Batalha and prepare measured drawings of it. Murphy began publishing these drawings in 1792, and in 1795 the full volume of *Plans, Elevations, Sections and Views of the Church of Batalha* was published in London. It was widely read by a number of leading architects, including Wyatt, and a German edition appeared in 1813. Accompanying the plates was an 'introductory discourse on the principles of Gothic architecture'. Murphy's plates certainly inspired the octagonal tower at Fonthill, but they came after Wyatt's tower at Lee Priory, although it is possible that Wyatt could have conferred with his patron Conyngham about Batalha.

In considering the architecture of Lee Priory, Walpole praised Wyatt's fidelity to Gothic models and his inventive powers in using those models, calling him a genius. Wyatt was to justify the praise of Walpole in the major commission of his career, Fonthill

*An illustration of the south end of St Michael's Gallery at Fonthill Abbey, Wiltshire, published in* John Britton's Graphical and Literary Illustrations of Fonthill Abbey, *1823. The oriel window was noted by observers as shedding a cheerful glow, enhanced by the stained glass. Beneath fan vaults, which derived from the cloisters of Gloucester Cathedral, sat a suite of ebony furniture, medieval and Renaissance metalwork, and part of Beckford's collection of rare books and manuscripts.*

Abbey in Wiltshire, the most romantic of Gothic houses for the most romantic patron of the Gothic Revival. In William Beckford, the charming but exasperating James Wyatt met his match. Beckford was the sensitive, highly intelligent son of a man who had made an immense fortune in business in the West Indies and who eventually became Lord Mayor of London. Young Beckford was bilingual in English and French, and spoke other languages as well. He had been briefly tutored in music by Mozart and was taught drawing by the well-known artist Alexander Cozens. He had also travelled widely on the Continent. The elder Beckford, in keeping with the taste of the day, had built a large mansion in the Palladian style in Wiltshire called Fonthill Splendens. This was where the young William Beckford lived from the age of ten to 36, when he moved into a remarkable Gothic house built for him by Wyatt.

Fonthill Splendens, during William Beckford's occupancy, had rooms decorated in a variety of antique styles. When Beckford decided to demolish his father's house, he remarked 'Forget the old palace … with all its false Greek and fake Egyptian.' In addition to Greek and Egyptian rooms, there was a richly decorated room in the Turkish style, which represented a minority taste during the eighteenth century; its use at Fonthill

*An illustration of the Entrance Hall at Fonthill Abbey, Wiltshire, published in John Britton's* Fonthill, *1823. One of the sublime experiences offered to visitors at Fonthill was entering the house through a 30-foot high pointed door and ascending the flight of steps beneath a timbered ceiling of darkened oak past tall, narrow lancet windows up to the Octagon Hall.*

*The Entrance Hall at Fonthill, published in Rutter's* Delineations of Fonthill and its Abbey, *1823. Rutter described how 'the atmosphere of the coloured light, and the solemn brilliance of the windows, produces an effect very little removed from the Sublime'.*

*Opposite: This view of Fonthill, seen from the north west, shows the tall, needle-like spire that was never built. This watercolour by Charles Wild of 1799 was completed shortly after Wyatt exhibited his designs for the abbey at the Royal Academy. The resemblance of the building's silhouette to nearby Salisbury Cathedral is obvious, and Fonthill was organized around a cruciform plan with one long and one short axis. This was truly 'abbey Gothic'.*

Splendens was a reflection of Beckford's fascination for the Middle East and its past. He had loved the *Tales of the Arabian Nights* as a boy and, in 1782, he began writing his own Arabian novel, *Vathek*, set in the medieval Islamic world. This could be described as a Gothic novel by virtue of its emphasis upon the supernatural and the use of an exotic, historically remote setting. Beckford was to publish several other works, including *Recollections of an Excursion to the Monasteries of Alcobaça and Batalha* in 1835, recounting his extensive travels in Portugal and his observations of its medieval architecture.

In his fascination for the remote past and for foreign cultures, Beckford shared the enthusiasms of many Romantics. Ever since he was a teenager, he had planned to add a Baronial Hall with stained glass and heraldic decoration to his father's mansion. About half a mile from Fonthill Splendens were the ruins of an important medieval friary, and Beckford conceived of building a 'Fonthill Abbey' on the site. Initially the abbey was intended as a rather splendid Gothic folly, not as a residence. His plans were interrupted by domestic troubles in 1793, when Beckford left for a three-year stay in Portugal.

The year before Murphy's book was published, Beckford had visited Batalha and then settled for the summer on the outskirts of the town of Sintra, the long-standing summer residence of the Portuguese court and a town which had delighted Byron for its rocky hills, pine forests, and medieval Moorish and Christian ruins. At Sintra Beckford rented the Quinta of Monserrate, a Gothic Revival castle with towers and a central octagon built a few years earlier for an English

resident. Beckford was so enchanted with the castle that he tried, unsuccessfully, to buy it for himself.

Before leaving England Beckford had consulted James Wyatt, who was then finishing Lee Priory, about building a Gothic abbey at Fonthill. Upon his return in 1796 the project began in earnest. By 1798 Wyatt was exhibiting a proposed view of Fonthill Abbey at the Royal Academy in London. This view featured a prominent octagonal tower with an elongated spire, a development upon the Octagon Wyatt had designed for Lee Priory. The enormous spire of Fonthill, resembling that at nearby Salisbury Cathedral, was never built, and the octagonal tower was hastily made in cement but collapsed in 1800. Even after it was rebuilt in stone, Beckford disagreed with Wyatt over the Gothic design of the balustrading within the tower, and reportedly kicked it, sending it crashing to the ground. The shabby building practices of Wyatt's team, owing to Wyatt's continual attempts to find construction short cuts and his failure to supervise his men properly, became a considerable irritant to Beckford and eventually poisoned his relationship with this talented architect.

The collapsed Octagon at Fonthill was rebuilt late in 1800 in time for a grand party given by Beckford for Admiral Nelson, the future hero of the Battle of Trafalgar. Beckford attached great importance to the occasion, set in his Gothic folly, as he hoped it would be the means of establishing himself as a host and party-giver to be reckoned with. He had gone to Portugal in 1793 to escape the increasing scandal surrounding the public knowledge of his homosexuality, which was not tolerated openly at the time.

The fact that Beckford had inherited an enormous fortune acquired by trade must also have inflamed public opinion against him.

In December of 1800 the splendid party for Nelson was held, attended by celebrities such as the American-born artist Benjamin West, then President of the Royal Academy, and Nelson's notorious mistress, Lady Hamilton, wife of the British consul in Naples. West, in particular, greatly admired the architecture of Fonthill Abbey, describing it as 'magical'. The guests stayed overnight at Fonthill Splendens but were treated to a Gothic banquet at Fonthill Abbey, for which carriages wound along the drive through an evergreen wood strung with lanterns. They dined at a 53-foot table in the 'Cardinal's Parlour', waited on by servants in medieval dress. Dinner was in the medieval style, 'unmixed with the refinements of modern cookery', as it was reported in the press, and afterwards Emma Hamilton entertained the company with her famous 'attitudes', or pantomimes. There was music from a minstrels' gallery throughout the evening. The party was to be typical of Beckford's career – spectacular, and executed on a lavish scale, but curiously remote from human warmth or friendship.

At the time of the party for Nelson, Beckford's intentions were that Fonthill Abbey be a garden folly and a place of entertainment on the grounds of his father's mansion, where he still resided. At some point he decided to make the abbey his principal residence, and in 1807 he moved in. It was as if he wished to make his fantasy become his reality. Work was still in progress at the time of Wyatt's death in 1813, and it proceeded for another five years. Although

 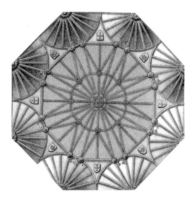 

*Three ceiling details at Fonthill Abbey, Wiltshire, in Rutter's* Delineations of Fonthill, *1823. Left: Star-shaped pendants of the Sanctuary. Centre: Fan and pendant vaulting of the Grand Saloon. Right: Flat rosette-shaped tracery of the Yellow Drawing Room. All of these can be traced back to the elaborate Decorated and Perpendicular Gothic styles of the fourteenth and fifteenth centuries in England. The Drawing Room ceiling is derived directly from the fan-vaulted cloister of Gloucester Cathedral.*

only a small portion of Beckford's abbey remains today, contemporary illustrations survive. The painter J M W Turner was engaged to sketch Fonthill in progress, and there were no less than six books published on the house, beginning in 1812.

The house was built on the plan of a cross, not unlike that of a medieval cathedral, with the Octagon centred above the crossing. A rectangular block protruded to form the vast entrance to the abbey on its western side, being approached by an avenue several miles long through the park. On the eastern side of the building was another rectangular block containing the principal reception rooms, while the northern and southern arms of the cross were long, relatively narrow 'galleries' built to house Beckford's enormous collections of books and manuscripts, antiquities, and objects of art, many of medieval date. In addition, the southwest quadrant of the building contained a fountain court ringed with other smaller structures, including 'Nelson's Turret', named for the admiral who had banqueted there. Architectural features such as windows and mouldings designed by Wyatt were varied but remarkably faithful to

medieval models. Some of the narrow lancet windows with dripstone mouldings in the Early English style of Gothic seem to have been taken directly from Salisbury Cathedral, where Wyatt had been busy with his controversial restoration.

The silhouette of the building, seen from a distance, was strikingly irregular and asymmetric, being dominated by the looming, central octagonal tower. High towers from which isolated figures looked down upon the world were part of Beckford's romantic vision, as illustrated by a passage in *Vathek* describing the Prince's feelings about the tower in his palace:

*His pride arrived at its height when, having ascended, for the first time, the fifteen hundred stairs of his tower, he cast his eyes below… The idea which such an elevation inspired of his own grandeur completely bewildered him.*

Despite the complex and convincingly medieval architecture by Wyatt, it was the immense size of the abbey and its tower that was the most remarkable feature of Beckford's Fonthill. The entrance door was 30 feet high, and to increase the sense of height, with characteristically dry humour, Beckford hired a dwarf as a doorman. In defining the Sublime, Burke had considered height the most powerful type of 'vastness'.

The Romantic poet Percy Shelley described a castle deep in the woods in his Gothic novel *Zastrozzi* (1810), and it is tempting to wonder whether Shelley was describing Fonthill. In the novel, the unsavoury Zastrozzi 'beheld a large and magnificent building, whose battlements rose above the lofty trees. It was built in the Gothic style of architecture, and appeared to be inhabited… A large portico jutted out: they advanced towards it and Zastrozzi attempted to open the door… It was a large saloon, with many windows. Everything within was arranged with princely magnificence.' Shelley went on to describe Zastrozzi's progress into a vaulted hall with a large flight of stairs leading into 'a lengthened corridor', until he unexpectedly met a sinister figure from his past who was the owner of the castle.

At Fonthill one entered a hall of tremendous height with a hammerbeam ceiling and stone tracery in the Early English style of Salisbury. Opposite the door was a large flight of stone steps leading into the Octagon underneath the tower. The Octagon opened onto the two enormous galleries, each over 100 feet long, named for St Michael and St Edward. These were decorated in a rich crimson, gold and purple scheme and contained a number of important books and works of art. The view from one gallery into another created a sublime vista extending the length of the abbey and may correspond to the 'lengthened corridor'

in Shelley's description. The vibrant colour schemes used at Fonthill were recorded in coloured illustrations published by Rutter and were to influence other Gothic houses like Eaton Hall, designed by Wyatt's pupil William Porden.

The poet Samuel Rogers, who was shown round Fonthill Abbey by Beckford himself in 1817, was dazzled by the galleries:

*On Mr B's stamping and saying, "Open!"*
*the Statue flew back, and the Gallery was seen,*
*extending 350 feet long. At the end an open*
*Arch with a massive balustrade opened to a vast*
*Octagon Hall, from which a window shew'd a*
*fine view of the Park. On approaching this it*
*proved to be the entrance of the famous tower –*
*higher than Salisbury Cathedral; this is not*
*finish'd, but great part is done. The doors, of*
*which there are many, are violet velvet covered*
*over with purple and gold embroidery.*

While the description of Rogers's visit may have exaggerated the actual size of the Fonthill galleries, it accurately conveys the sense of scale and richness that overwhelmed visitors to the abbey and that had characterized Wyatt's architecture from the beginning of his career.

Beckford became a virtual recluse during the time he inhabited Fonthill, and visitors to the house were infrequent. However, the public were able to view the foremost Gothic Revival house in Britain when it was prepared for sale at auction by Christie's. During the summer of 1822, some 7,200 people bought tickets to view Fonthill. The public opening of the abbey enabled John Britton and John Rutter each to publish a book describing the house and

*Oak woodwork in the Chapel at Ashridge House, Hertfordshire, 1806–c1818. The house was designed by James Wyatt with assistance from Jeffry Wyatville. Where Fonthill was sublime, Ashridge was scholarly. The details of the immense house were observed from medieval sources and crisply executed, sometimes lending the house a dry, slightly lifeless character.*

its collections. This, in conjunction with the sale catalogue compiled by Christie's, greatly increased the influence of Fonthill on architecture and interiors of the time.

In the end it was typical of Beckford that he decided to sell the house privately to a Mr Farquhar for £350,000, an enormous sum, before the auction could be held. Nonetheless, the eccentricity of Beckford himself, the sale of his romantic abbey and the dramatic collapse of its central Octagon three years later in the storm, all led to heightened public awareness of Fonthill and of the possibilities of architecture in the Gothic style. Fonthill was not Wyatt's only

vast and imposing Gothic Revival house, but it was without doubt his most romantic one.

Of a less dramatic and more scholastic character was Ashridge Park, sited on a high ridge on the border between Hertfordshire and Buckinghamshire. It is the only major Gothic Revival house by Wyatt that still stands today, although it is no longer a private residence. In 1806 Wyatt had begun Ashridge for the Earl of Bridgewater. Like Fonthill, it was a house of gigantic proportions on the site of a medieval monastic foundation. Whereas Fonthill was in appearance vertical, Ashridge was horizontal. The entire entrance façade, including the service

*A view from the Gallery of the Great Hall at Ashridge House, Hertfordshire, 1806–c1818. One of the most notable features of Ashridge is its exquisitely worked stone details. When Wyatt began work on the house, he was also supervising the restoration of Henry VII's Chapel in Westminster Abbey, whose signature motifs of the portcullis and the Tudor rose appear above the traceried frieze.*

*Opposite: Like the timbered ceiling in the Entrance Hall of Fonthill, Wyatt's timbered ceiling at Ashridge harks back to late medieval examples such as those at Hampton Court and Westminster Hall. The enormous scale of the Great Hall – it is 95 feet high – is comparable with the architecture of Fonthill.*

*A detail of the Stair Hall at Ashridge. The sculpted saints in canopied niches depict the founders and benefactors of the thirteenth-century monastic college in whose grounds the house stood. The college had been closed down during the Dissolution of the Monasteries under Henry VIII.*

blocks, was over 1,000 feet long. Prince Pückler-Muskau admired the park, which he described as 'one of the largest in England', but he was less than enthusiastic about the architecture of the house:

*The house which … is modern gothic, is almost endless, with all its walls, towers, and courts. I must however frankly confess, that this modern gothic style which looks so fairy-like on paper, in reality often strikes one not only as tasteless, but even somewhat absurd from its overloaded and incongruous air.*

The view of posterity of the house is kinder than that of Pückler-Muskau, for Ashridge is recognized as having anticipated the archaeological direction that the Gothic Revival was increasingly to take during the first half of the nineteenth century. Wyatt was able to draw upon the services of Thomas Gayfere, the mason whose skills were being used for the contemporary restoration of Henry VII's Chapel at

Westminster. Wyatt's Gothic details, observed from his restoration work, gave Ashridge a convincingly fifteenth-century character. The plan was asymmetric, like Wyatt's other Gothic houses, with a cloister on the right of the main entrance, above which was a large square block with Perpendicular Gothic windows, dripstone mouldings, battlements, clustered chimneys, and small lateral octagonal turrets. As with Fonthill, the Entrance Hall gave onto an astonishingly high Great Hall of 95 feet, entered through a stone screen with three Perpendicular arches.

Lord Bridgewater owned a quarry nearby, so stone was used more lavishly for details of the house than it had been at other Wyatt houses. The Stair Hall of Ashridge was remarkable for its Gothic details, featuring canopied niches with statues of figures linked to the history of the house. Above the stairs rose a light well decorated with mock fan vaulting, and all the windows and openings were arranged in clusters of

*An early nineteenth-century view of Pakenham Hall (later Tullynally Castle), Co. Westmeath, Ireland. This was an eighteenth-century house that had been Gothicized in about 1800. The architect, Francis Johnston, an admirer of James Wyatt's Slane Castle, Co. Meath (c1785), added battlements and round towers. In about 1845 Richard Morrison considerably enlarged the house by adding two wings. The result was a very horizontal and somewhat irregular façade.*

three Perpendicular arches. The original reception rooms had oak panelling with gilt details, and the walls were hung with crimson damask. However, despite the overwhelmingly Gothic character of the exterior, chapel, entrance and stair hall, the main reception rooms of the house were designed in a more or less Baroque style, in accordance with the wishes of the patron. The only Gothic feature of the reception room interiors was the traceried windows, which were in harmony with the exterior.

Wyatt died suddenly in 1813, leaving Ashridge unfinished. Fortunately, he had several sons and a nephew in the architectural profession who were able to succeed him. Wyatt's nephew Jeffry, later to become Sir Jeffry Wyatville, worked on the house for another six years. He had already been involved in the design of the Entrance Porch, the chapel, and a number of the interiors, as well as designing Gothic furniture. Wyatville's was clearly a superior talent in the Gothic style. In 1814 Benjamin Dean

Wyatt, one of James's sons, designed a bench for the Entrance Hall of Ashridge with a rather conventional eighteenth-century shape. The back was ornamented with repetitive cusped lancets and a trefoil frieze. Of much greater interest, however, is an octagonal table designed by Wyatville in 1815 for the Entrance Hall. The design was based upon a medieval baptismal font, with a massive octagonal base decorated with simple recessed lancets. The top was supported by traceried brackets, and the design had a sense of weightiness about it. The form was derived from a real medieval source, and this adoption of ecclesiastical design to suit domestic purposes was typical of Gothic during the Regency period.

Of the large Wyatt family, Jeffry Wyatville was its most successful member. He died a wealthy man with numerous honours, having been knighted and having 'gentrified' his name. In 1828 at the height of his career Wyatville was painted by the leading portraitist of the day, Sir Thomas

*Details of a skylight (left) and a fire surround (right) at Tullynally Castle, Co. Westmeath, Ireland. These rather thin and linear Gothic designs date from about 1800 when the house was Gothicized by Francis Johnston. The use of flower-like forms is typical of eighteenth-century Gothic design.*

Lawrence, with the silhouette of Windsor Castle looming in the distance and plans for the Round Tower beside him on a table. Wyatville added considerable height to the Round Tower in order to make the silhouette of Windsor more picturesque. The remodelling of Windsor was his most important commission and one that won him the admiration of George IV.

George III, who had appreciated the medieval architecture of Windsor, had hired James Wyatt to re-Gothicize the castle. The work was never completed, but Wyatt's exterior lancet windows and Gothic stair hall remain today. Wyatt had also designed and partially built a Gothic palace at Kew for George III which featured the technically innovative feature of an internal, 'fireproof' skeleton of cast iron. Kew Palace was entirely demolished by George IV, who concentrated his energies on making Windsor the principal seat of the monarchy during his reign.

Windsor Castle is the only residence of the modern British monarchs to date from the Middle Ages, when it was built as a fortified residence to protect the medieval kings and strengthen their hold on the surrounding territory. The Baroque architect Hugh May, working for Charles II late in the seventeenth century, had extensively remodelled what was then an ageing, decrepit complex and created a suite of lavish Baroque state rooms. All but three of these were replaced by Wyatville during the 1820s remodelling. Most of Wyatville's interiors were in the 'old French' manner beloved of George IV – that is, they were essentially reviving the Rococo style of the *ancien régime* in France. However, it was recognized at the time that the only appropriate style for the exterior and public areas of Windsor Castle, the symbolic centre of the ancient British monarchy, was the Gothic. Perhaps the only thing on which James Wyatt and John Carter were agreed was that Gothic was the 'national style'. The nationalistic associations of the Gothic with the monarchy's long history in the British

*An illustration of the staircase at Windsor Castle, Berkshire, 1800–04, by James Wyatt, published in Pyne's* Royal Residences *of 1817–20. Windsor Castle is the only surviving medieval royal residence. George III, an enthusiast for Gothic architecture, hired James Wyatt to restore the Castle in the Gothic style between 1800 and 1804. Here Wyatt's carefully observed details of slender colonettes, leaf capitals and ribbed vaulting with bosses came straight from the medieval cathedrals he was restoring, most notably, Salisbury Cathedral.*

Isles did not escape George IV, who was wary of French Revolutionary ideas finding their way across the Channel. Nor was the statement made by Windsor Castle lost upon contemporary observers from the Continent.

The remodelling of Windsor in the 1820s encouraged a public appetite for the Gothic that had been whetted by the sale of Fonthill Abbey. A German visitor, J D Passavant, commented that Wyatville's alterations to Windsor 'are executed on a scale of the greatest magnificence and in such perfect keeping with the antique character of the building, that Windsor Castle may now be considered as the finest royal residence in England.' He praised Wyatville's

taste in designing in the Gothic style. Prince Pückler-Muskau, an astute observer in matters of taste and design, was even more effusive, in a letter to his wife in Germany describing his visit to Windsor:

*This morning we visited the Castle, which is now completing according to the old plan, and is already the vastest and most magnificent residence possessed by any sovereign in Europe.*

Fonthill Abbey and Windsor Castle were the most prominent examples of a group of imposing Gothic Revival houses and castles constructed during the early nineteenth century. These tended to fall into one of

*Designs for Candelabra for Windsor Castle, by A W N Pugin, 1827. At the age of 15, Pugin was already recognized as a prodigy in terms of design. His designs for standing light fixtures for the Dining Room and Gallery of Windsor Castle were elegant by the standards of the 1820s. They were later repudiated by him when he criticized his adaptation of ecclesiastical architectural forms such as crocketted pinnacles for interior domestic use.*

two categories originally identified by the eighteenth-century poet William Shenstone: monastic and castellated architecture. These were taken up and popularized by the Regency landscape architect Humphrey Repton, who remarked that monastic, or 'abbey' Gothic, was appropriate for flat sites and fertile valleys, while castellated, or 'castle' Gothic, was to be used for an elevated site with nearby dramatic landscape features such as cliffs or rocky outcrops.

Wyatt's Ashridge can be seen as a rather grand example of monastic, or abbey Gothic, with its long, relatively low silhouette on a flat ground. Wyatt also designed a group of private castles, as did two Crown Architects, John Nash and Robert Smirke, who were best known for their classical architecture. Smirke's Eastnor Castle in Herefordshire, begun in 1812 on the site of a medieval castle, is an outstanding example of the 'castle Gothic' style illustrated in Repton's publications. The plan was essentially

symmetrical and based upon the quadrangle, although variety and interest was given to the silhouette of the castle by means of corner turrets, battlementing, and a raised central block. While the design was not innovative, Eastnor sat extremely well on its elevated site and gave a highly picturesque impression.

Somewhere in between monastic and castellated architecture was Eaton Hall in Cheshire, a large Gothic house by William Porden, the pupil of James Wyatt, who was at work for the Earl of Westminster between 1804 and 1812. The rich red used for the walls of the reception rooms of the house, along with deep blue curtains and patterned carpeting, must have been inspired by Wyatt's schemes for the interiors of Fonthill Abbey, especially the famous Galleries. In the Eaton Hall Saloon this vivid colouring contrasted with the stone coloured fan vaulting and the traceried windows, a Gothic decorative treatment with a long history extending back to the Gallery of Strawberry

*'Design for a Pavilion and Green House for a Gothic Mansion', published in Humphrey Repton's* Observations on the Theory and Practice of Landscape Gardening, *1803. Repton considered the Perpendicular Gothic style used here to be appropriate for greenhouses and conservatories because it allowed for broad windows which would admit a great deal of light.*

Hill. Like Fonthill, Porden's Eaton Hall was famous for its size, for its sumptuously decorated interiors, and for the inhospitable chill which reigned inside the house regardless of the weather outside.

It is difficult to gauge the effect of the house today, as it was demolished in the 1860s to make way for a later Gothic Revival house. In 1826 the architect J C Buckler published a limited colour edition of *Views of Eaton Hall*, which illustrates the principal reception rooms. Pückler-Muskau described in some detail his reaction to Porden's Eaton Hall:

*We hastened to see the wonders of Eaton Hall, of which, however, my expectations were not very high. Moderate as they were, they were scarcely realized. The park and the gardens were, to my taste, the most unmeaning of any of their class I had seen, although of vast extent; and the house excited just the same feeling in me as Ashridge, only with the difference that it is still more overloaded, and internally far less beautiful, though furnished still more expensively, in patches. You find all imaginable splendour and ostentation which a man who has an income of a million of our money can display; but taste not perhaps in the same profusion. In this chaos of modern gothic excrescences, I remarked ill-painted modern glass windows, and shapeless tables and chairs, which most incongruously affected to imitate architectural ornaments. I did not find one single thing worth sketching; and it is perfectly inconceivable to me how M Lainé could, in the Annals of the Berlin Horticultural Society, prefer this to any he had seen; at which indeed his English critics have made merry not a little …All the magnificence lay in the gorgeous*

*'Design for a Conduit Proposed at Ashridge' by Humphrey Repton, published in* Fragments on the Theory and Practice of Landscape Gardening, *1816. The crisp architectural detail of this design, with its flying buttresses and crocketted pinnacles, made it highly suitable for the gardens of Ashridge, where Wyatville was finishing the house designed by his uncle, James Wyatt.*

*Eaton Hall, Cheshire, from the south-east, published in J C Buckler's Views of Eaton Hall, 1826. William Porden, a pupil of James Wyatt, was the architect of Eaton Hall (1804–12) for Lord Grosvenor. The style of the exterior was essentially Decorated Gothic of the fourteenth century. Despite the lavish ornamented detail used in its design, and the vast scale of the house, critics felt its architecture was rather dry and lifeless.*

*Opposite: An illustration of the Saloon published in Buckler's Views of Eaton Hall, 1826. While Porden's Eaton Hall compares with the Gothic interiors of Fonthill and Windsor, it nonetheless failed to impress critics favourably on account of the profusion of small-scale ornaments in contrast with the large scale of its rooms. The house lacked the discipline of Wyatt's Gothic interiors.*

*materials, and the profuse display of money. The drawing-room or library would, for size, make a very good riding-school.*

The first Eaton Hall can be seen as a kind of apogee of the Gothic style during the Regency period, in which the tremendous scale and rich ornamentation introduced in the capable hands of James Wyatt were less successful when copied by lesser talents. In addition to Porden, another designer who was much influenced by James Wyatt's Gothic was George Smith, the self-proclaimed 'Upholder Extraordinary to His Highness the Prince of Wales', who published designs for Gothic furniture and interiors between 1808 and 1826. Smith's designs display the same overloaded and ecclesiastical character that was criticized by Pückler-Muskau and by later Gothic Revivalists, most notably A W N Pugin.

Before the excesses of Regency Gothic could be corrected, accurate information concerning the visual and architectural characteristics of real, medieval Gothic architecture had to be made available. James Wyatt's Gothic was convincing in design terms because it was inspired directly by his work at medieval sites like Salisbury Cathedral and Westminster Abbey. During the first half of the nineteenth century, book production became cheaper and an outpouring of books and illustrations of Gothic architecture made familiarity with medieval models easier to acquire. Whereas the revival of the Gothic style in the eighteenth century had been reserved for those members of the upper classes with the means for architectural experimentation, this explosion of literature was to make the Gothic style increasingly available to owners of ordinary, middle-class houses.

*Design for a Gothic Cottage, published in Humphrey Repton's* Fragments on the Theory and Practice of Landscape Gardening, *1816. The cottage was designed as if it were a single 'cell' of Repton's 'abbey-style' architecture. Emphasis has been given in the design to crocketted pinnacles along the roofline and massive stepped buttresses on the four corners of the central block. The cottage would have been a suitable residence for an estate employee.*

Neither has the Gothic been confined to the cathedral ... but its beauty and picturesqueness have reappeared in the Old English styles of domestic architecture. The most perfect examples are those of the castles and mansions of England of the time of the Tudors, but the whole of the cottage architecture of England is imbued with its spirit, and the manifestations are every-where visible. *Andrew Jackson Downing,* Cottage Residences *(1842)*

*Design for a Castellated Villa, published in E Gyfford's* Designs for Elegant Cottages and Small Villas, *1806. Gyfford described the design as 'particularly well adapted to the romantic scenery in the north and west of England'. Certainly, the combination of a bold, round tower on the left with a battlemented block on the right creates a startlingly asymmetric and picturesque design.*

From the 1790s books of designs for domestic architecture aimed specifically at the middle classes began to appear. Gothic designs were included in these pattern books from the start. One of the earliest examples must be John Crunden's *Convenient and Ornamental Architecture*, first published before 1791, when a new edition was issued.

In the 1760s, Crunden had been involved in the publication of several pattern books for decorative art, including furniture and ornamental features. His designs included the Gothic and Chinese styles. *Ornamental Architecture* was his first purely architectural book of designs and, while the majority of these were in a classical or even Palladian style, designs for Gothic houses do appear. The full title of the book suggests that Crunden hoped for a wide audience: '*Consisting of Original Designs, for Plans, Elevations, and Sections: Beginning with the Farm House, and Regularly ascending to the most Grand and Magnificent Villa; Calculated both for Town and Country, and to Suit all Persons in every Station of Life*'. It is clear that he was chiefly addressing the middle classes, although he felt his designs would suit people in 'every station of life'. In his

preface he said he wanted his designs to be 'very clear and intelligible to gentlemen and workmen'. Indeed, his book was meant to be a practical building guide. Crunden gave dimensions and explanatory notes with each design, as well as specific measurements for ideal room proportions: ceiling heights for the ground floor, or parlour storey, containing the principal reception rooms, should be ten to 14 feet high, while the chamber storey, normally the first floor, in which the bedrooms were contained, should be nine to 12 feet, depending upon the grandeur of the scheme adopted and the means of the builder of the house. Crunden also advised that those on a limited budget should be sparing in the use of ornament and that, while stone was much preferred for use on the exterior, grey brick or even stucco could be an acceptable alternative.

In the same practical vein but with superior Gothic designs was the slightly later *Designs for Elegant Cottages and Small Villas* ('*Calculated for the Comfort and Convenience of Persons of Moderate and of Ample Fortune*'). This was published in 1806 by the designer E Gyfford, who trained at the Royal Academy. Gyfford's book goes so far as to include estimates of cost for each design if built (£500 was the price for a standard four-bedroomed cottage), and each plate was accompanied by commentary. The styles used were Grecian and Gothic, 'wherein elegance and utility blended with the equally-important consideration of economy, might be acceptable'. This was clearly design for the bourgeoisie.

It is interesting to note that the term 'bourgeois' has lengthy associations with the Gothic style in architecture. It was first used

*The Fish-keeper's Cottage at Port Logan, Scotland, c1820. This design in rough, whitewashed stucco bears similarities to the asymmetry of Gyfford's castellated villa. The availability of pattern books with Gothic designs in the first half of the nineteenth century led to the creation of a folk genre in the Gothic.*

in northern France in the fourteenth century to refer to the merchant and middle classes who were beginning to build impressive stone houses in the Gothic style previously reserved for cathedrals and ecclesiastical architecture. It seems fitting that the bourgeoisie should have taken up the style again during the Gothic Revival of the nineteenth century. The designs of Crunden and Gyfford were very much a part of this phenomenon of Gothic for the middle classes.

Gyfford stated categorically that he wished to give 'the importance of the villa to the cottage, not the cottage character to the villa.' In other words, his designs were aimed at making the grander appearance of a country house available to those who could only afford a cottage. He pointed out that it

was not appropriate to make a larger, more imposing residence look like a cottage. His audience was the aspiring middle class, and clearly he was out of sympathy with the self-effacing, pseudo-rustic cottages introduced by the architect John Nash at Blaise Hamlet to create a picturesque landscape. Gyfford's commentary does, however, indicate his awareness of contemporary aesthetic ideas, as seen in his use of terms like 'picturesque' and 'romantic'.

In the illustrations of his Gothic residences, Gyfford's designs display the battlements, pointed gables and lancet windows fashionable at the time. Plates 7, 8 and 9 illustrate a four-bedroomed Gothic cottage of which Gyfford remarked that 'the pointed heads of the windows breaking into the roof, contribute in no inconsiderable degree to the

effect which produced in this design a very picturesque appearance.' In fact, the 'cottage' in Plate 8 had a distinctly ecclesiastical, or 'abbey', character owing to its blind tracery, Latin crosses and large pointed arch window.

A somewhat larger house, a Gothic villa with five bedrooms, two dressing rooms and a water closet, was illustrated in Plates 13 to 15. This was of a more castellated appearance, having battlementing, round side towers with crosses, and narrow pointed lancets. Gyfford remarked that this castellated villa had 'an ancient or Gothic character, and … [was] particularly well adapted to the romantic scenery in the north and west of England'. Grander still was the seven-bedroom villa (one bedroom to house a state bed) illustrated in Plates 21 and 22 'for the comfort of a small family:

*… The castle style adopted in this design affords, if the situation and circumstances are well chosen, a pleasing and interesting character*

*… The effect produced by variety of forms, and of light and shadow, to those who are admirers of this style [will win their approbation].*

In his use of the term 'castle style' and in his references to the site of a building modifying, if not determining, its architectural style, Gyfford can be seen as a popularizer of the most advanced design ideas of the day, most notably those of Humphrey Repton, which he translated into workable patterns for the middle-class market. This was to become a burgeoning trend in nineteenth-century publishing. In 1806, the year in which Gyfford published his *Designs*, Repton published his third book, *An Inquiry into the Changes of Taste in Landscape Gardening*, eventually followed by the very influential *Fragments on the Theory and Practice of Landscape Gardening* in 1816, one of the major design publications of the early nineteenth century. Although some of the houses illustrated by Repton were

*'Elvills, Englefield Green – Seat of the Hon W H Freemantle, MP', 1822, published in Ackermann's* Repository of the Arts, *vol. IX, plate 14. With its setting on low ground next to a body of water, the house illustrates Repton's idea of 'abbey' Gothic. Visually, the design stresses the horizontal rather than the vertical, while the repeated use of pointed lancet windows and arches at ground level suggests an abbey cloister.*

by no means palatial, the architecture and surrounding grounds he illustrated were well beyond the reach of the ordinary person. Many middle-class Gothic enthusiasts would have turned instead to Crunden or Gyfford for guidance in building a Gothic house.

The phenomenon of the middle-class Gothic villa was well established in Britain by the time Prince Pückler-Muskau was travelling around the country. In 1826 he described a villa in Stanmore, Hertfordshire, which he praised far more enthusiastically than he had Wyatt's Ashridge or Porden's Eaton Hall. The villa was:

*…thoroughly in the rural-gothic style, with ornamented pointed gables; a 'genre' in which English architects are peculiarly happy. The interior was also most prettily fitted up in the same style, and at the same time extremely comfortable and inviting. Even the doors in the walls surrounding the kitchen-garden were adorned with windows of coloured glass at the top, which had a singular and beautiful brilliancy among the foliage. The little flower-garden, too, was laid out in beds of gothic forms surrounded by gravel walks, and the fancy had not a bad effect.*

This Gothic villa is the sort of residence prescribed by Gyfford's book where, in keeping with Repton's country house design, even the very modest garden of a suburban villa was seen as an integral part of the design of the house.

Neither Crunden nor Gyfford offered much advice on the furnishing and decorating of the Gothic interior. Since the first edition of Thomas Chippendale's furniture pattern book had appeared in 1754, a limited number of designs for Gothic-style furniture had been available. However, many more Gothic designs for furnishings and interiors became available with the

*Design for a Gothic whist table and chair, by A C Pugin, 1827, published in Ackermann's* Repository of the Arts. *The table reveals the influence of Continental Gothic in its pierced frieze of mouchettes. Despite its back in the form of a rose window, the chair is really a disguised 'klismos', or neoclassical chair type popular at the beginning of the nineteenth century.*

publication of Rudolph Ackermann's well-known magazine of design in the Regency period, *The Repository of the Arts*. This was issued from 1808 by Ackermann, a German immigrant coach designer, from his London shop. Ackermann's was a kind of design emporium where clients could get ideas for furnishing schemes in a variety of current styles. In the early years of the *Repository*, George Smith's designs for Gothic furnishings were prominent, with such notable ideas as a Gothic state bed raised on a dais (no doubt suitable for Mr Gyfford's seven-bedroom castellated villa) and a baby's cradle thick with crocketted pinnacles and tracery.

Among Ackermann's employees was a group of Frenchmen who had fled the Revolution and subsequent political upheaval. The best-known of them was Augustus Charles Pugin (the father of the

famous Gothic Revival architect) who was employed in Britain as the draftsman for the Crown architect John Nash. Beginning in 1825, A C Pugin's designs for Gothic furnishings regularly appeared in Ackermann's magazine, and he became one of the most important topographical artists of the first half of the nineteenth century. He gave special attention to publishing accurate illustrations of the medieval buildings of Britain, beginning with the influential *Specimens of Gothic Architecture* (1821–2), which was published by John Britton and included a glossary of medieval architectural terms.

Britton himself was a figure of considerable influence in the Gothic Revival of the early nineteenth century through his incessant publishing activity. Two of his series, *The Architectural Antiquities of Great Britain*

*Design for a Gothic Saloon by Gaetano Landi, 1810, published in* Architectural Decorations. *Landi was born in Bologna, worked in London, and published a book of designs in a variety of styles. This interior is distinguished from contemporary English examples by its aggressive angularity.*

(1807–26) and his *Cathedral Antiquities* (1814–35), became standard reference works concerning architecture of the Middle Ages. These tomes, together with Ackermann's *Repository*, made sources for Gothic Revival design more widely available and contributed to a greater awareness of its elements, among craftsmen, builders, and middle-class clients. As the art historian Kenneth Clark has remarked, 'Though Britton's volumes were a commercial venture, they did not merely feed a craze; they gave the average cultured man a far truer idea of Gothic forms than he had hitherto had.'

The problem that remained for the early Gothic Revivalists, however, was the paucity of accurate information about medieval architecture, and it was for another arrival on the Gothic scene to write the first clear, accurate account of the characteristics

and development of Gothic style in the Middle Ages. This was Thomas Rickman, a Quaker accountant working in Liverpool who had become interested in medieval architecture while wandering through churchyards in grief after the death of his wife. The first edition of his essay, *An Attempt to Discriminate the Styles of English Architecture from the Conquest to the Reformation*, was published in 1817, and the seventh and final edition was in 1881; it became the standard text on Gothic architecture throughout the nineteenth century.

In the preface to his first edition, Rickman stated that he intended his book to be 'a text-book for the architectural student', as the lack of such a book on medieval architecture 'is generally acknowledged'. His object was to supply 'at a price which shall not present an obstacle to extensive

*Opposite: Design for the Fitzwilliam Museum, Cambridge, by Thomas Rickman and R W Hussey, 1835. Rickman and his assistant submitted three designs for the Fitzwilliam competition, two of them with enormous towers. Here Gothic features can be traced back to Wyatt's design at Fonthill with its accurately observed details and 'sublime' silhouette. Rickman's* Attempt to Discriminate the Styles of English Architecture *was a best-selling handbook in the nineteenth century. For the first time ever it set forth, clearly and simply, an accurate account of the development of Gothic architecture.*

*A pair of cottages in Wells, Norfolk, early nineteenth century. Here the height of the ground floor enabled the anonymous builder of these cottages to install properly pointed, lancet-shaped windows. The upper storey windows had to be less pointed, however. The random pattern of the brickwork is most unusual and distinct from the formal patterning demanded by classical styles.*

circulation' an overview of British architecture to assist restorers and builders. His audience was the same as that of Ackermann, Britton and A C Pugin, but he went beyond these men in terms of the simplicity of presentation and art historical accuracy of his text. Rickman was able to categorize the ornamental features he observed on medieval churches, and the result was a clear, readable and affordable text-book to explain Gothic architecture to the layperson.

To set the book into context, there had been great confusion amongst antiquarians since the seventeenth century over the origins of the Gothic. The architect of Eaton Hall, William Porden, agreed with Christopher Wren that the Gothic was Saracenic, or Islamic, in origin. John Carter, a relentless critic of James Wyatt, insisted that the Gothic was English in origin. The geologist

Sir James Hall worked out an elaborate theory to demonstrate how Gothic architecture had developed from primitive architecture of wicker and wood. Hall's *Essay on the Origin and Principles of Gothic Architecture* was first published in 1797 and expanded in a second edition of 1813. Soon afterwards his book was superseded by Rickman's. To test his theory Hall built a small cathedral of wicker, complete with large traceried windows and a spire, in his own garden. This curiosity disappeared long ago, but Hall's *Essay* reminds us how sensible and pragmatic Rickman's approach to the Gothic really was.

Rickman was able to succeed in his *Attempt* where those before him had failed, perhaps owing to the skills of 'discrimination' he developed during his career as an accountant. His notebooks, which are now in

*The stone Entrance Porch at Painswick, Gloucestershire, c1825. The archaeological character of this porch, with its crisply executed battlements, stepped buttresses and dripstone mouldings, places it within the 'archaeological' phase of the Gothic Revival. This was a period when textbooks such as Rickman's were changing the character of Gothic design.*

*A doorcase in Lonsdale Square, Islington, London, 1838–45. This doorcase, designed by R C Carpenter, in white stucco, with its frieze of quatrefoil lights and its wooden door of vertical boarding, illustrates how Gothic features (in this case the Perpendicular Gothic) were adapted to modest town architecture during the second quarter of the nineteenth century.*

the Bodleian Library in Oxford, are packed with hundreds of examples of ornamental and architectural features sketched at a large number of Gothic sites. Rickman was able to organize these sketches into the categories he devised, and to analyze the results. For example, he noticed that medieval windows had four basic shapes: round-headed with geometric ornament; narrow and sharply pointed; more broadly pointed with decorative tracery; and very broad, with hardly any point at all and grid-like tracery. Eventually he worked out the sequence of English medieval architecture and defined the terminology we still use today as Norman, Early English, Decorated and Perpendicular. By studying medieval buildings of more than one period, Rickman developed for the first time an accurate chronology of English medieval architecture, progressing from Anglo-Saxon, to Norman, to Gothic. He

suspected that the Gothic had originated in France and regretted his lack of opportunity to study French architecture at first hand.

By 1820, then, pattern books for building modest residences in the Gothic style were available, along with an accurate text concerning the development and ornamental features of Gothic architecture. The adoption of Gothic by the middle classes had begun. In 1833 a Scottish landscape architect named John Claudius Loudon published a lengthy volume that was quickly to become the Bible of middle-class building and garden design. Loudon's *Encyclopedia of Cottage, Farm and Villa Architecture*, which was followed by supplements and later editions, was arguably the most popular and influential publication on design of the nineteenth century, and much of its success must be credited to its practical, even utilitarian, approach.

*A print illustrating Plas Newydd, near Llangollen, Wales, mid-nineteenth century. In 1780 two well-born first ladies, Lady Eleanor Butler and Sarah Ponsonby, moved into a medieval cottage in Wales and re-named it Plas Newydd. Between 1798 and 1814 they added oriel windows with stained glass and oak carvings to the entrance porch to Gothicize the house.*

In the preface to the first edition of his *Encyclopedia*, Loudon remarked that a knowledge of architecture was not widespread among the general public, and he looked forward to a day when architecture and design would be included in general education. It is especially interesting that Loudon suggested that designers and builders should turn away from the ancient and classical civilizations as sources for designs and, instead, look to those closer in time and location. He did, however, include designs for the 'Grecian' style in his book, along with Gothic, Tudor, Swiss, Italian, and other styles. In keeping with his mission to bring good design to a wider audience, Loudon recommended useful books for further reading, including Rickman's *Attempt*,

the *Specimens* of A C Pugin, Richard Payne Knight on taste and the Picturesque, and T F Hunt's book on *Tudor Architecture* of 1830, a subject of great interest to antiquarians at the time.

Book One of Loudon's *Encyclopedia* contained 'Designs for Labourers' and Mechanics' Cottages, and for Gardeners and Bailiffs, and Other Upper Servants, and for Small Farmers and Cultivators of their own Land'. There were designs for five-room cottages, cottages for a husband and wife without children, and a block of six cottages grouped together so as to be economical to build. Plate 28 illustrates an attractive Gothic-style residence, 'A Cottage in the Old English manner containing a Kitchen, Living Room, and two Bed Rooms', on an

*An illustration of Gothic windows in wicker and stone, published in Sir James Hall's* Essay on The Origins and Principles of Gothic Architecture, *1797, plate XI. Hall's* Essay *was based on the premise that Gothic architecture originated from trees and the wicker architecture of the early inhabitants of the British Isles. These twin Gothic arches in wicker and stone provide a good illustration of Hall's theory.*

asymmetric, L-shaped plan and an exterior with two pointed gables and an oriel window. More imposing, and illustrated in Plate 31 was 'A Dwelling with Five Rooms, with Conveniences, in the Old English Style, where the building material is chiefly Stone.' Loudon remarked that this handsome Gothic house would be very suitable for a gardener or bailiff. Farm buildings, schools, and 'hovels for cattle' were all included, making the *Encyclopedia* invaluable for anyone charged with running an estate.

The influence of Loudon's publications was enormous and not confined to the British Isles. In 1814, on a tour of European parks, Loudon visited Moscow, where his ideas received attention from a Scottish architect named Adam Menelas, who worked for the Czars. Menelas began to build Gothic landscape architecture and country retreats in the Gothic style in Russia, perhaps the most famous of which was Nicholas I's country residence in Petershof, known as 'The Cottage'. The interiors were organized around a Gothic stair hall, as Strawberry Hill had been, and the house had Gothic style furniture whose design was supervised by Menelas.

Loudon's publications had their greatest overseas influence, however, in North

*A view of 'Willow Cathedral' by Alexander Carse, c1794. In an attempt to test his theory that Gothic architecture derived from wicker architecture, Sir James Hall had a miniature wicker 'cathedral' built in his garden. It is seen here under construction.*

America. Canada was still a British colony and therefore British architectural ideas were current. In the new Republic of the United States, the legacy of British culture was, likewise, still strong. Moreover, those who lived and worked in the countryside, who constituted the majority of the population in the nineteenth century, rarely had money available for lavish building, unlike the wealthy merchants who lived in the established cities of the eastern seaboard. With the opening up of the interior of the United States and the spread of the population westwards during the nineteenth century, a sizeable market for practical architectural and design pattern books was created amongst the more prosperous settlers and farmers. Loudon's *Encyclopedia* was read widely in the United States, and his ideas were re-cast in an American mould by Andrew Jackson Downing.

It would be fair to say that A J Downing brought the Picturesque to North America. He had trained as a gardener in New York State and began to gather ideas for books on landscape gardening and rural architecture late in the 1830s. He was greatly influenced by Loudon, and in 1842, at the age of 27, he published his second book, *Cottage Residences*, in which were included 15 designs for cottages and villas in landscape gardens. Most were for the well-to-do, but one design was a 'Cottage for a Poor Country Clergyman'. Downing defined the cottage as

'a dwelling so small that the household duties may all be performed by the family', while 'a villa is a country house or larger accommodation, requiring the care of at least three or more servants.' He noted that American clients could not generally afford houses as large as those in Britain, so that the cottage rather than the villa was often a more appropriate domestic form for the new republic.

Later, in *The Architecture of Country Houses* (1850), Downing wrote that he wished to give 'some little assistance to the popular taste' in building, for the villa was the instrument of a man of 'easy income, who builds a villa as much to gratify his taste, as to serve the useful purposes of a dwelling.' The middle classes of Republican America should not waste time, he said, 'in the vain effort to transplant the meaningless conventionalities of the realms of foreign cast'. Not for Americans were the grand country houses such as Fonthill, Ashridge, or Eaton Hall. An American domestic architecture was to be modest and practical. Downing continued, 'Another serious objection to this imitation of the elaborate architecture of villas in small cottages, is the

impossibility of executing the ornamental parts in a proper manner.' He may also have had in mind the difficulty of finding craftsmen in North America who were trained in the use of the Gothic style, as most had never seen the medieval monuments of Europe.

The sort of Gothic dwelling Downing envisioned for a person of modest income was illustrated in Design IV, 'A small Cottage of Brick and Stucco, in the Gothic Style'. This attractive design had an L-shaped plan, which Downing observed would please those who favoured picturesque design, along with a triple lancet window in its gable, a bay, and pointed windows in the bedrooms. While the cottage was modest in its pretensions, Downing remarked that it was nonetheless 'expressive of architectural style'. In a similar vein was Design VI, 'A Gate-Lodge in the English style'. 'The chief merit of this cottage is its picturesqueness', being sited within a 'fine group of trees'. The lodge had a verandah, leaded pane windows of varying size, and a varied and irregular silhouette. Downing commented 'The style of this design is the rural Gothic, that beautiful modified form of Gothic architecture which

*Design for 'a Villa in the Pointed Style', by A J Davis, c1840, published in A J Downing's* Cottage Residences *(1842). Davis, the most prominent American Gothic Revival architect, supplied a number of designs for Downing's influential pattern books. This villa was built for a client in Albany, New York.*

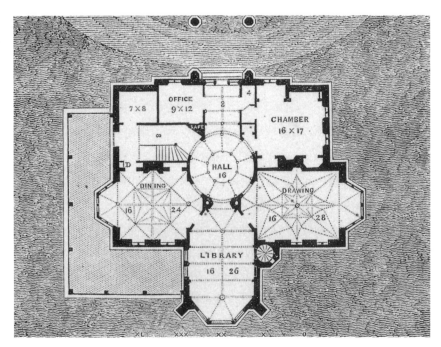

*Opposite: A detail of the chimneypiece in the Sitting Room at Carriglass Manor, County Longford, Ireland, by Daniel Robertson, 1837–40. The design includes crisp details and a broad perpendicular arch. This is close to contemporary English designs such as John Soane's chimneypiece for the Gothic Library at Stowe, Buckinghamshire.*

*An interior and exterior detail of a traceried window at Carriglass Manor. The original Jacobean house was rebuilt in the Gothic style for the future Lord Chief Justice of Ireland. Here the tracery designs take the form of lopsided mouchettes. The Gothic details of the house are highly original.*

we adopt from the English people; and which certainly expresses as large a union of domestic feeling and artistic knowledge as any other known.' From such designs published by Downing was descended the 'stockbroker's Tudor' architecture of the early twentieth century that characterizes so many American suburbs.

Perhaps the most significant contribution of Downing to American domestic architecture was that he stressed the importance of a useful, well-functioning house. He frequently used the Gothic style to meet these criteria, while appreciating the inherent picturesque quality of the Gothic. Downing's influence might have been even greater if his career had not been cut short by his early death in a steamboat accident in 1852. Nonetheless, the importance of his ideas was felt throughout the nineteenth century in North America, not least because of the work of a colleague, Alexander Jackson Davis.

Davis was a New York City architect who created an American Gothic style for villa and cottage architecture. He worked in a variety of styles but was particularly adept in the Gothic, supplying designs for

Downing's publications from 1839 to 1852. Davis excelled in the 'Rural Gothic' that was recommended by Downing, and he is credited with having designed the first American Gothic villa (as opposed to the first Gothic townhouse, 'Sedgeley' in Philadelphia, by Benjamin Latrobe in 1799). Davis's pioneering villa was Glen Ellen in Maryland, designed in 1832. Six years later came his most important early Gothic house, Knoll, situated in Tarrytown, New York.

Knoll was part of a whole group of Gothic houses built along the Hudson River Valley for artists, writers, successful businessmen and public servants. These were often country retreats for New Yorkers who wanted to escape the noise and heat of the summer. Davis's client was William Paulding, a distinguished public servant and congressman who had been a General in the War of 1812. Paulding was a relation by marriage to the writer Washington Irving, who had employed Davis in 1837 to Gothicize his own house, Sunnyside. It was probably due to Irving's recommendation that Paulding engaged A J Davis as the architect for his Gothic villa, Knoll, in the following year.

*A watercolour study for the Rotch House, New Bedford, Massachusetts, by Alexander Jackson Davis, 1845. The design displays several distinctive features which are typical of American Gothic, such as the use of a porch, or verandah. This was originally advocated by A J Downing, with whom Davis worked closely. The lively, sinuous design of the tracery with quatrefoils and cusping is characteristic of Davis's Gothic style.*

*Delamater House, Rhinebeck, New York, by A J Davis, 1844. The design closely resembles that of the Rotch House, with the exception of the use of the wooden board and batten siding advocated by Downing.*

*Ericstan, Tarrytown, New York, by A J Davis, 1855. Davis built a Gothic castle of stone high above the Hudson River for J Herrik, a wealthy merchant. The round tower on the left housed a parlour vaulted from a central pier with radiating ribs in the manner of the famous polygonal chapter houses of English cathedrals, such as Wells in Somerset.*

Knoll was completed in 1842. As its name suggests, the house was situated in an elevated position overlooking the Hudson. It was cruciform in plan and strikingly asymmetric in its architectural details, with varied windows, a high gabled entrance porch, and a verandah to the south balanced by a battlemented tower to the north. Of the Knoll interiors, the Library was one of the most important. To Downing, the Library of a villa served as the seat of culture, an idea going back to the eighteenth century. At Knoll, Davis adapted the plate for a Gothic library with a dramatic timbered ceiling which was illustrated by the Gothic Revival architect E B Lamb in Loudon's *Encyclopedia* of 1833.

By English standards, Knoll was a small villa in keeping with the scale of Gyfford and Loudon's designs. In 1864 Davis was called back to enlarge the house for a new owner, George Merritt, for whom he added a four-storeyed tower and a new dining wing with a three-storeyed oriel. The larger house was renamed Lyndhurst, as it is still known today. Merritt evidently wished to educate himself about architecture and design, as Davis prepared a reading list of over 200 items for him, including Payne Knight, Repton, and Loudon. Other important sources for Davis's work were Rickman's *Attempt* and A C Pugin's *Specimens*, from which he culled ornamental features for his designs. The resulting exterior of Lyndhurst had a variety of pleasingly Gothic details of the Early English, Decorated, and Perpendicular styles set forth by Rickman. Window treatments – in particular, tracery – seem to have been a focus of Davis's interest.

The guiding hand of Davis was seen in the interiors of Knoll/Lyndhurst, as well. In the 1840s alone, Davis designed about 50 items of furniture for Knoll. His Oak Saloon, or drawing room, chair featured a round back shaped like the traceried rose window of a medieval cathedral with cusped arches attaching the caned seat to the legs. The hall chair design, while also executed in oak with a caned seat, had a triple lancet back again based on window tracery with details of cusping and crocketted leaves. The later furniture by Davis, such as the oak chairs designed for the new dining wing at Lyndhurst, displays greater solidity of form and a more simplified silhouette, while still retaining the use of crockets, cusping, and tracery motifs.

A J Downing had remarked that 'A Gothic character may easily be given to plain chamber furniture by any joiner or cabinet-maker who has tools to make the necessary mouldings.' The design of Davis's Gothic furniture went far beyond the simple addition of mouldings to ordinary forms, but other more commercial manufacturers in the United States certainly followed Downing's advice. In the nineteenth century American craftsmen and builders produced some extraordinary examples of Gothic churches, cottages and furnishings embellished with fanciful wooden ornaments, a folk genre of great charm that has come to be known as 'carpenter's Gothic'.

Davis was not the only architect to build Gothic residences in America at this time. As early as 1835 the British-born architect Richard Upjohn designed a bold, stone, castellated house named 'Oaklands' for Richard Gardiner of Gardiner, Maine. In 1839 he began his most famous work, a delightful summerhouse in the Gothic style for a Savannah, Georgia, businessman named George Noble Jones. This was in Newport, Rhode Island, later to be described in *American Mansions and Villas* of 1883 as 'the Eden of watering places, and the summer home of many distinguished persons'. Jones's cottage was on the outskirts of the town, which was even then famed for its colonial architecture.

The original building was on a small scale, like Davis's Knoll. Although there was little of the Gothic inside the house, the exterior was designed with a variety of gables and dripstone mouldings above casement windows on the ground floor and leaded windows on the first floor. The plan was asymmetric, with a recessed entrance under a projecting bay with a gable. The building was wooden but painted grey to imitate stone. It acquired its name, Kingscote, when it was purchased in 1864 by William King. Kingscote was subsequently enlarged in the 1870s to transform the summer cottage of Upjohn into a villa.

While the effect of Kingscote is highly picturesque, Upjohn's Gothic architecture is less convincingly medieval in character than that of Davis as his ornamental forms were more generalized. By contrast, the exterior of Knoll, as seen in Davis's drawings in the Metropolitan Museum in New York, had crockets, clustered chimneys, and a battlemented tower all recognizably drawn from medieval architecture. In addition, many of Davis's country villas such as Knoll

*Opposite: The Entrance Hall of Lyndhurst, Tarrytown, New York, 1838–42, enlarged in 1864–7. Originally called Knoll, Lyndhurst was Davis's most important early Gothic villa, for a distinguished public servant, William Paulding. In the Entrance Hall the vaulting is reminiscent of that of James Wyatt, with its narrow bays, steeply pointed arches and sparse but well-articulated ornaments. The wheel-backed chair, its shape echoing that of a Gothic rose window, was designed by Davis in 1841 for the Drawing Room.*

*Opposite: The
'Wedding Cake' House,
Kennebunkport, Maine,
c1800, with Gothic details,
c1850. One of the more
spectacular uses of American
'carpenter's Gothic', this
house was created by
encasing a plain, classically
inspired house in a wooden
outer shell of Gothic
details. The extravagant
design includes enormous
crocketted pinnacles and
elaborately traceried perpendicular arches. A large
cusped ogee arch was used to
frame the original Palladian
window above the entrance.*

*Kingscote, Newport,
Rhode Island, by Richard
Upjohn, c1839, enlarged
c1870. The pronounced
variety and asymmetry of
the façade of Kingscote
place it within the tradition
of the Picturesque. Richard
Upjohn, who was born in
Britain, used a far more
generalized variety of
Gothic detailing than that
of Davis. Upjohn provided
plans and instructions for
making simple Gothic
elements in wood in his book*
Rural Architecture *(1852).*

were executed in stone, which greatly
enhanced their medieval character. Davis
also designed cottage residences in wood,
the more usual building material in North
America, and he is credited with having
refined the vertical wooden siding known as
'board and batten' that is found on so many
American wooden structures. However, it
was Richard Upjohn, through publishing
*Rural Architecture* in 1852, who provided
plans and detailed instructions for making
simplified Gothic features in wood, thus
promoting the adaptation of the British
Gothic villa to American materials.

It can be seen, therefore, that A J Davis
was ahead of his contemporaries in terms
of the medieval appearance of his designs,
which were closely linked to British models.
While his façades generally display a convincing Gothic character, details of his work
such as his tracery motifs appear to be highly
individual interpretations of Gothic. This is
not surprising in a country where medieval
architecture was non-existent.

Certain analogies can be drawn between
American Gothic and contemporary Gothic
in Ireland, where a very different medieval
tradition led architects to create a distinct
version of the Revival imported from
England. In the first third of the nineteenth
century, when a great number of Irish
country houses were built, Richard Morrison
and his son William Vitruvius Morrison
were two architects who designed a group of
country houses in an eccentric but pleasing
and highly picturesque form of Gothic.
James Wyatt, who had a prominent
commission for a Gothic castle in Ireland, is
often credited with having inspired the
Morrisons' work in the style.

Perhaps one of the most romantic
Gothic structures by the Morrisons was
William Morrison's Brittas Castle in County
Tipperary. This was begun after 1820, when
an ancient castle on the site was destroyed by
a fire. The owner, Major Langley, engaged
Morrison to build him a massive, baronial
style replacement for the lost original.

The unfortunate Major was killed by falling masonry on the site in 1834 and work ceased, leaving only the gateway of the new castle. This survives as a sad monument to Langley's antiquarian passions. Judging from its ruined gateway, Brittas would have been a splendid and imposing castle with massive octagonal turrets, a parapet, and narrow archers' windows overlooking a moat, all giving the air of a castle keep in a novel by Sir Walter Scott.

Castle Howard in County Wicklow is perhaps more typical of the Morrisons' country house architecture in the Gothic style, as it was designed in several medieval styles to look as though it had grown over time. Richard Morrison, the father of William, had received the commission to Gothicize the small, plain, existing house when it was purchased by a new owner, Mr Howard, in 1811. The new 'Castle Howard' was designed in a combination of the abbey and castle styles made popular by Repton. The highly asymmetric exterior has a tall, gabled block flanked by stepped buttresses joined to a battlemented tower. The exterior details include traceried windows, dripstone mouldings and a projecting porch in keeping with the tradition of Wyatt. However, the decoration inside the house was more similar to the Gothic of the eighteenth century. A spectacular circular stair hall features Perpendicular Gothic windows flanked by ogeed niches in plasterwork that seem to have come straight from Batty Langley's pattern books. At the top of the stairs hangs a giant plasterwork pendant modelled after the Chapel of Henry VII at Westminster and used in so many eighteenth-century Gothic houses in England. The rich lacelike detailing is an unexpected contrast to the crisply modelled stone exterior.

*The exterior of Castle Howard, Co. Wicklow, Ireland, remodelled by Richard Morrison after 1811. The combination of doubled round towers, clustered chimneys and raised battlements displays a pleasing variety in its use of Gothic forms, linking it to picturesque aesthetics.*

Cottage and villa architecture came to Ireland in about 1830, shortly before it reached North America. William Morrison was engaged by the Duke of Northumberland to build Lough Bray Cottage at about this date for a physician, Philip Crampton, who had supposedly cured the Duke of a skin problem. It was a picturesque design in a Tudor-like style with oriels and clustered chimneys, set on the shores of Lough Bray. More imposing, and also in County Wicklow, was the stone villa of Hollybrooke, designed and built by Morrison around 1830 for the painter Sir Robert Hodson but finished for his brother, George, also a painter and an amateur architect. The asymmetrical façade features a large and boldly projecting entrance porch with a Perpendicular arch, above which rises an attractive traceried oriel window. The Stair Hall has rather eccentric but effective woodwork in narrow pierced lancets underneath a timbered ceiling, the whole very much in keeping with the spirit of the somewhat dry detailing of Wyatt's Gothic houses, although on a more modest scale.

By means of pattern books and antiquarian texts, then, a modest, domestic version of Gothic Revival architecture was developed in England and spread to other countries. Particularly in North America, a kind of folk or vernacular Gothic style was developed. The builders and carpenters who used books like Downing's as the basis for their own experiments in the Gothic style often worked for clients who lived in remote countryside locations where professional architects were either unaffordable or unavailable.

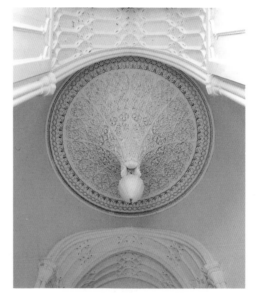

*The Library and Sitting Room (below right) at Castle Howard. Many unusual varieties of Gothic forms can be seen in these interiors. While the shape of the door-cases looks back to Batty Langley's designs, the use of ogees on the door panels themselves is highly original. Shamrocks have been carved into the fireplace just underneath its battlemented 'turrets', and the flattened tracery of the ceiling is also original in its execution, if not its conception.*

The increasingly common appearance of modest yet fanciful Gothic designs for the ordinary person in the first half of the nineteenth century gradually provoked a reaction amongst architects and antiquarians, who feared the debasement of the style. The result of this was a search for greater accuracy and archaeological correctness in Gothic design, accompanied by moral and religious concerns.

*A detail of polychromy in the Chapel of the Blessed Sacrament, Church of St Giles, Cheadle, Staffordshire, 1841–6. Crace and Son executed the painted decoration, under the supervision of the architect A W N Pugin. Of all Gothic Revival architects, Pugin probably came closest to capturing the spirit of medieval architecture in work such as this.*

An unwavering faith, a most singular piety towards bygone ages, a veneration the most profound for all that appertained to the beauty of the courts of The Lord, an imagination glowing with the glories of the past, all combined in impelling the subject of this memoir to surrender his heart and soul to the desire for the restoration of the forgotten faith and for the revival in the land of its ancient magnificence in art and architecture. *E S Purcell on A W N Pugin (1861)*

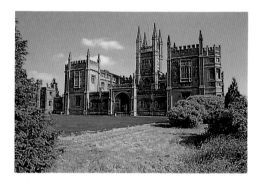

Early in the nineteenth century, a new type of Gothic design based upon the careful study of medieval architecture began to rise to prominence. This development had been foreshadowed in the eighteenth century by Walpole's later work at Strawberry Hill and Newdigate's alterations to Arbury Hall. However, the antiquarian stream of the Gothic Revival intensified during the first half of the nineteenth century while the authors of popular pattern books were churning out designs for ornamented cottages and villas. Following Rickman's *Attempt* of 1817 came a stream of publications representing the increasingly scholarly concerns of Gothic Revivalists. Antiquarians had interested themselves in the Gothic since the seventeenth century and were the first patrons of eighteenth-century Gothic. However, with the growing popularity of the Gothic during the first half of the nineteenth century, and the increasing freedom with which builders and craftsmen interpreted the style, it was inevitable that Gothic enthusiasts of a scholarly frame of mind should wish to reform what they viewed as travesties of the style.

One of the earliest champions of scholarly Gothic architecture was, at first

glance, quite unlikely. He was Charles Hanbury Tracy (created first Baron Sudeley in 1838), the son of a man whose fortune derived from the Pontypool Ironworks in Wales. Among the public offices he held, Hanbury Tracy served as a Whig MP for Tewkesbury for ten years. Upon his marriage to his cousin in 1798, he settled in his wife's family seat, Toddington Manor, Gloucestershire. He eventually decided to rebuild the Jacobean house after it had been damaged by fire in 1800. By 1819 Hanbury Tracy had designed an impressive and convincingly Gothic house as his new seat. The date of the original house was early seventeenth century, but the characteristics of this period in architecture were understood at the time as late Gothic. 'Tudor' architecture, which encompassed the Jacobean period, had only recently been defined by Rickman and was linked to Perpendicular Gothic. Hanbury Tracy therefore chose the Perpendicular style for the design of Toddington.

It is not clear where Hanbury Tracy could have received training in architecture, a subject for which he had a natural talent. Like many early Gothic Revivalists he was educated at an Oxbridge college – in his case, Christ Church, Oxford. This may have sparked his interest in the Gothic, which he considered to be the appropriate choice for his family seat as the lineage of the Tracy family could be traced back to one of the assassins of Thomas Becket. It is known also that Hanbury Tracy considered Gothic to be the most suitable style of architecture for the British climate.

Contemporary accounts leave no doubt that Hanbury Tracy himself was the architect of Toddington, no matter how little formal

*A detail of the cloister vaulting at Toddington Manor. The elaborate 12-part vaulting of the cloister was capped by finely carved stone bosses based upon medieval sources. Here Satan seizes an unfortunate sinner.*

training he may have had. In 1837 the *Gentleman's Magazine* described the new house thus: 'The curiosity of those who take an interest in architecture has been much excited by the erection of a magnificent mansion, not many miles from Cheltenham, the owner of which has been his own architect.' At about the same time Mrs Arbuthnot, the friend and confidante of the first Duke of Wellington, recorded in her Journal that Hanbury Tracy 'is entirely his own architect and, unlike other gentleman architects, seems to have built what will be a very comfortable as well as a good house.' This generous praise was justified, and John Britton, the antiquarian publisher who had published a volume on Fonthill Abbey, saw fit to devote an entire volume to Toddington Manor in 1840.

The Gothic architecture of Toddington is remarkably archaeological in character for its early date. The foundation stone of the house was laid in 1820, and much of the shell of the building was complete in 1823. The plan was centred on a courtyard containing a square tower with crocketted pinnacles. The exterior was executed in yellowish Cotswold stone with the liberal use of oriel windows, battlementing and pinnacles along the roofline. On the east the lower service and stable ranges, also battlemented and arranged on courtyards, created a pronounced asymmetry of plan which was emphasized by a second tower above the stable entrance. The exterior architectural details of Toddington are noteworthy for their superior workmanship, the carving and tracery of the Chapel exterior being especially fine. One name among the craftsmen is known, that of J C Lough, who carved some of the sculptural programme

*A detail of the oak panelling at Toddington Manor, Gloucestershire, 1819-23. Hanbury Tracy favoured the Late Gothic styles of Decorated and Perpendicular. The striking effect of the quatrefoils and cusped ogee arches seen here is created by the crisp articulation and three-dimensional modelling of the ornamental details.*

of the house and later created the tombs of Hanbury Tracy and his wife.

The quality of the architectural details at Toddington was excellent, and exemplified by the cloister surrounding the quadrangle of the house on all sides. The colonettes in the cloister have beautifully carved leaf capitals in the medieval manner, with corbelled heads below dripstone mouldings over the door and window openings. The stone vaulting gives a splendid effect with its 12-part division and finely rendered leaf bosses. The model was Hanbury Tracy's Oxford College, Christ Church; Magdalen College, Oxford, was the prototype for the central tower at Toddington.

The medievalism of the Toddington architecture was deliberately varied in order to make the house appear as though it had been added to over the centuries. This was not a completely new feature; James Wyatt had designed Fonthill Abbey in several distinct styles of medieval architecture to create the same effect for William Beckford. Wyatt's variety of styles may have had more to do with the inclination for picturesque effect, however, than the more antiquarian impulse which seems to have governed Hanbury Tracy's architecture.

Comparisons can also be drawn between Toddington and the architecture of Thomas Rickman, the author of *An Attempt*, who built a beautiful little Decorated Gothic church of local stone early in the 1820s for the Lucy family of Warwickshire. The church at Hampton Lucy has exquisitely executed Gothic details such as a battle-mented parapet, a square west tower, corbelled heads and stiff leaf capitals, all comparable in their medieval quality to the

*The ceiling in the Dining Room at Toddington Manor, Gloucestershire, 1819–23. The richness of the ornamental details at Toddington gave the house a remarkably vivid Gothic character for its early date. The Dining Room ceiling may owe its inspiration to Crosby Hall in London which was an important source for Gothic Revivalists in the first half of the nineteenth century.*

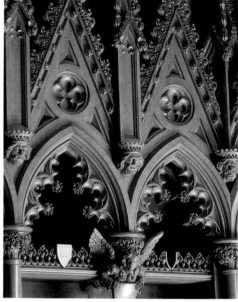

*The Library at Toddington Manor. The winged angels above the bookcases are taken from those in the famous Late Gothic timbered ceiling of Westminster Hall, London.*

contemporary work at Toddington Manor. In the mid-1830s, when the interiors at Toddington were being finished, Rickman tried to please a difficult client at Matfen Hall, Northumberland, by designing, 'on the supposition that a building of earlier date had existed the Hall of which being found in sufficiently good condition has been retained and a house of later character built round it.' This was to become a noticeable feature of antiquarian Gothic houses. Rickman himself, in *An Attempt*, had pointed out that careful examination of medieval structures often revealed they had been built over several centuries with differing architectural features.

The most elaborate of the Toddington interiors were the Dining Room and Library. The former was a large room, some 40 by 20 feet, with a coved timbered ceiling with carved pendants and gilt detailing. The doors

of the room were topped with Perpendicular arches and blind arcading surmounted by heraldic shields. The style of most of the architecture at Toddington was Perpendicular Gothic, the latest of medieval styles. However, the Library featured rich Decorated Gothic tracery in wood on the bookcases, which were topped by steeply pointed gables with quatrefoils flanked by crocketted pinnacles. When taken as a whole, the richness of the exterior and interior ornamental details of Toddington gives an unusually vivid Gothic character to the house. Designed in 1819, it ranks as the first major monument of the new phase of the Gothic Revival in which a more literal, archaeological approach was to dominate.

Perhaps more than any other building of the Gothic Revival, it was the New Palace of Westminster, the complex containing the Houses of Parliament, that captured the

*The exterior of the Palace of Westminster, London, c1835–65. Charles Barry was the architect of the new government complex at Westminster, the seat of the Houses of Parliament and the first major public building of the Gothic Revival. A W N Pugin assisted Barry with the design of ornamental details and the interiors.*

imagination of the public on an international scale. Parliament buildings from Ottawa to Budapest were to follow the lead of Westminster in using the Gothic style to symbolize the medieval origins of the parliamentary system. The old Palace of Westminster complex was composed of medieval structures dating back to the late eleventh century with additions from the modern period, including Gothic elements in stucco designed by James Wyatt. However, the entire complex was destroyed by a fire in October 1834. (This was recorded in spectacular fashion in a painting by Turner.) According to legend, it was the tally sticks from the Office of the Exchequer that acted as tinder, lighting the Thames for miles in each direction. Only a handful of medieval structures, most notably the magnificent Westminster Hall, originally the Great Hall

of the Norman kings, survived the blaze. What was undoubtedly a national tragedy in terms of the loss of a rich medieval heritage also became an opportunity for those Gothic enthusiasts with an archaeological bent.

Charles Hanbury Tracy chaired the commission to select the designs for rebuilding the palace. He was a supporter of the winning design by Charles Barry, which offered some striking similarities to the architecture of Toddington and suggests that Barry may have consulted Hanbury Tracy. First, there was the asymmetrical placing of towers in the exterior of the Westminster design. The Victoria Tower, being square, traceried, and topped with crocketted pinnacles at its four corners, resembles an enlarged version of the tower at Toddington. Second, the Perpendicular Gothic seen in the exterior of Toddington

The Central Lobby at the
Palace of Westminster,
1835–c65. The magnificent
Lobby designed by
Charles Barry (architect)
and A W N Pugin (interior
designer), situated below the
central spire, marks the
crossing point between the
long and short axes of the
plan, which was influenced
by Wyatt's Fonthill. The
splendid compass rose in
its centre was created by
Minton's, who supplied the
encaustic tiles for the Palace,
to mark the crossing where
one can gaze east into the
Commons Chamber or west
into the Lords' Chamber.

was also the style used for the exterior of the Palace of Westminster. Barry was not known for his proficiency in the Gothic style, and the most visible models available to him would have been Wyatt's prodigy houses of Fonthill, recently collapsed, and Ashridge, and Hanbury Tracy's Toddington.

Nor was Hanbury Tracy's activity as an architect over by the time he chaired the commission for selecting a design for Westminster. Between 1835 and 1840 he was closely involved in designing alterations in the Gothic style to the largest medieval manor house in Britain, Hampton Court, Herefordshire – not to be confused with the sixteenth-century palace built by Cardinal Wolsey on the Thames. Hampton Court in Herefordshire was built in the fifteenth century by a survivor of the Battle of Agincourt, and it had received castellated towers early in the eighteenth century from its owner, Lord Coningsby. In 1714 the antiquarian William Stukeley wrote that he had taken part in a medieval-style banquet at Hampton Court in which the diners were serenaded by minstrels while they ate. Early in the 1790s the south front of the manor house was remodelled in the Gothic style for the owner Lord Malden, and this was probably the work of James Wyatt, who was then occupied at Hereford Cathedral nearby, supervising its restoration in his capacity as Crown Surveyor.

It is almost certain that Wyatt's pupil, William Atkinson acted as an architectural consultant for the programme of modernization at Hampton Court, but it was Charles Hanbury Tracy who designed the architectural details. Hanbury Tracy was descended from a relation of the former owner of

Hampton Court, Lord Coningsby, so it is natural that he would have been interested in the house for its family connection as well as for its antiquity. The programme of remodelling in the 1830s was undertaken for John Arkwright, the grandson of the famous inventor, who had been introduced to Hanbury Tracy by a mutual friend. He had visited Toddington but thought its interiors dark and lacking in grand reception rooms. When Arkwright consulted William Atkinson about his plans for remodelling Hampton Court, the architect warned him, 'Do not make Hampton Court a cell to the Abbey of Toddington'. This was a clear reference to Hanbury Tracy's role in the remodelling of the house.

Nonetheless Arkwright proceeded, with Hanbury Tracy's help. The painstaking attention to detail typical of the latter's medievalism is seen in the remodelled south front with its rather elaborate Decorated and Perpendicular Gothic tracery in stone. The north front was more severe in appearance, as Arkwright wrote to Hanbury Tracy that he wanted to keep the old tower and the battlements there. Both Arkwright and Hanbury Tracy were very concerned to preserve the medieval character of the house while making improvements conducive to modern living. The different ranges of the house were united by means of a cloister, as at Toddington, a feature already established by James Wyatt in his remarkable Gothic houses. The interiors of Hampton Court made use of simple but effective medieval details such as tracery and decorative vaulting.

When taken in its entirety, the architectural activity of Charles Hanbury Tracy,

beginning with Toddington in 1819, encompassing the selection of designs for the new Palace of Westminster and ending with final improvements to Hampton Court in 1841, is an indicative example of the sharp rise in antiquarian activity during the 1820s and 30s in Britain that was to alter the character of Gothic Revival architecture and design.

One current that fed this antiquarian stream of development was the growing trade in antiques. During the first half of the nineteenth century, Continental Europe experienced profound political and economic disruption, beginning with the French Revolution and ending with the final defeat and exile of Napoleon in 1815. By contrast, Britain remained politically stable and wealthy. Thus British antiquarians were in a position to profit from the art and antiques available from displaced European collectors who needed to turn their assets into cash. Antique collecting was, of course, not new to the nineteenth century, but the scale of dealing in London during the first half of that century was without precedent. An antiques trade that is still in place today

began to flourish in the area between Soho and Bond Street.

The world-famous writer and Gothic enthusiast, Sir Walter Scott, who is best remembered for pioneering the genre of the historical novel, continued the trend established by Walpole and Beckford of filling his house with antiquarian objects and using Gothic and medieval elements to signify antiquity. Scott's house, Abbotsford, was located on the bank of the River Tweed in Scotland. In 1812, when Scott purchased it, it was a small house with a classical portico. The house was remodelled by him in conjunction with William Atkinson, the same architect who was to help remodel Hampton Court, Herefordshire. Other experts in Gothic design, such as the architect Edward Blore, assisted Scott when needed. By the year of Scott's death in 1832, Abbotsford had been transformed into a turreted and battlemented exercise in the Scottish Baronial style that attracted tourists from all over Europe and America.

Scott's novel *Ivanhoe*, published in 1819, was set in the twelfth century when

*A lithograph of the Eglinton Tournament, published by Day and Haghe, 1839. The staging of the Eglinton Tournament by the Earl of Eglinton, inspired by a passage in* Ivanhoe *by Sir Walter Scott, reflects a contemporary interest in realism in the depiction of medieval life.*

Richard I was returning to Britain from the Crusades and the old Anglo-Saxon and new Norman nobility resented one another. The character of Robin Hood plays an important part in the plot. *Ivanhoe* was the first Gothic novel to turn away from the Romantic horror genre pioneered by Horace Walpole and popularized by Ann Radcliffe towards a new realism in the depiction of medieval life. The vivid descriptions of castles, banquets and tournaments contained in the novel captured the public imagination of the day – so much so that the Earl of Eglinton decided to hold an actual medieval-style jousting tournament along the lines of that described by Scott in *Ivanhoe*. This was at his castle in Ayrshire, Scotland, in August 1839, seven years after the death of Scott.

Reportedly, some 80,000 people attended the event, including a large contingent of the press. Many of those attending, including some of the leading society figures of the day, wore splendid medieval costumes. Entertainment was in the form of tilting in armour, and a 'Queen of Beauty' was elected, just as described in *Ivanhoe*. The art historian John Steegman has described the Eglinton Tournament as 'the fancy-dress of Chivalry' and 'one superb Gothic outburst'. Certainly it illustrates the extent to which the medieval period had captured the public imagination by the 1830s. This was in no small part due to the success of Scott's novels and poetry.

Another Scott novel, *Kenilworth*, was set at Kenilworth Castle in Warwickshire, a ruin since the Civil War. Prince Pückler-Muskau found himself deeply affected by the ruins of Kenilworth, which he described to his wife thus:

*A plate from* Ivanhoe *by Sir Walter Scott (1840 edition). This illustration shows Rebecca, whom Scott used as the model for a courageous and spirited Romantic heroine in his most famous medieval story.*

*A portrait of Sir Walter Scott, 1832, after a painting by Henry Raeburn. Scott was a pioneer of the genre of the historical novel and his detailed portrayal of medieval life in* Ivanhoe *marked a departure from the Romantic emphasis on emotions and supernatural occurrences characteristic of earlier Gothic novels.*

*With Sir Walter Scott's captivating book in my hand I wandered amid these ruins, which call up such varied feelings. They cover a space of more than three-quarters of a mile in circumference, and exhibit, although in rapid decay, many traces of great and singular magnificence. The oldest part of the castle, built in 1120, still stands the firmest, while the part added by Leicester is almost utterly destroyed … and the whole surrounding country has a more barren, deserted and melancholy aspect than any part we have travelled through. But this harmonizes well with the character of the principal object, and enhances the saddening effect of greatness in such utter decay.*

The castle had strong associations with Elizabeth I, who had stayed there in the six-teenth century while visiting her childhood friend, Robert Dudley, the Earl of Leicester. Dudley's wife died suddenly at the castle, and his enemies claimed he had arranged her murder with a view towards becoming the husband of Elizabeth. With this emotionally-charged plot, it is not surprising that the historical novel should have been turned into a highly successful opera in 1831. In particular, the historical accuracy of the costumes and stage scenery were much discussed by contemporaries. The latter was the work of a teenager named Augustus Welby Northmore Pugin.

A W N Pugin stands as the towering figure of the Gothic Revival. He was born in 1812 to a French Catholic emigré, Auguste Charles Pugin, and an English Protestant,

*The frontispiece of*
Pugin's Gothic Furniture
*by A C Pugin, assisted by*
*A W N Pugin, published in*
Ackermann's Repository
of the Arts *(1827). The*
*elder Pugin contributed to*
*Ackermann's highly*
*influential magazine during*
*its final three years of*
*publication, from 1825 to*
*1828. The use of highly*
*ornamented, traceried forms*
*drawn from ecclesiastical*
*architecture was typical of*
*the approach to the Gothic*
*during the 1820s and 30s.*

Pugin's Gothic Furniture.

Published by R. Ackermann, 96 Strand.

Catherine Welby, the daughter of a well-to-do barrister. He was a child prodigy in terms of architectural drawing, and he began his professional career in 1827 designing for the King at Windsor. Throughout his life he travelled and collected antiquarian objects, including medieval manuscripts, which informed his work in the Gothic style. He became the most passionate champion of the Gothic, and his publications had an enormous influence upon designers during the second half of the nineteenth century. He died prematurely at the age of 40, having literally worn himself out with work.

Pugin's father, who had worked for the Crown architect John Nash, published the highly successful *Specimens of Gothic Architecture* early in the 1820s, and began publishing designs for Gothic furniture in Ackermann's *Repository* in 1825. There is evidence to suggest that his talented young son may have assisted Pugin *père* in designing in the Gothic style. An informative and sympathetic account of Pugin's life was written by his friend and contemporary, Benjamin Ferrey, an architect who trained alongside Pugin in his father's office. In his *Recollections of Pugin* of 1861, Ferrey recounts the curious contradiction between the personality of Pugin's father, who was sociable, refined and fun-loving, and that of his mother, who emerges from Ferrey's account as an intense and highly intelligent woman, staunchly Protestant and deeply ambitious for her son, with whom she had a close relationship.

Ferrey describes the harsh daily routine for young apprentices in the Pugin household, which was run by Catherine Welby Pugin. Apprentices were expected to rise at

six and to begin work before breakfasting at eight. The working day ended at eight o'clock at night, with two hours 'free' before bedtime. In addition to observing this routine, the young Pugin was expected to accompany his mother to long services on Sunday mornings at her church. Ferrey suggests that it was this strict upbringing which partially explains Pugin's rather colourful, bohemian adult life. However, there were frequent expeditions to the Continent, especially France, for young Pugin in the company of his parents. The father retained a group of artistic friends in Paris, and the son's upbringing was cosmopolitan.

The sophistication of Pugin's talent is evidenced by the fact that he successfully designed Gothic-style furniture for George IV at Windsor in 1827 at the age of 15. Ferrey informs us that 'The King took a lively interest in this matter, and resolved that those portions of the interior which retained a medieval character should be furnished with objects designed in a corresponding style.' The King's French upholsterer, M Morel, spoke to his compatriot, the elder Pugin, about obtaining Gothic designs for the Windsor furniture. The result was that A W N Pugin designed a suite of furniture in rosewood and gilt for the Windsor State Dining Room, made by the firm of Morel and Seddon.

Later, in his mature period, Pugin rejected his Windsor designs as incompetent examples of Gothic. This was because he had used fashionable contemporary forms for his pedestal sideboards and upholstered '*bergère*' chairs, which were based upon a popular type of French eighteenth-century

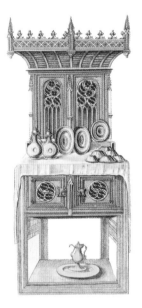

*Opposite: The frontispiece in A W N Pugin's* The Glossary of Ecclesiastical Ornament and Costume, *1844. Pugin's passionate interest in the Gothic extended from architecture across the full spectrum of the decorative arts, to the very dress of clerics in the 'true faith' of the Catholic Church. In formal terms, Pugin's emphasis upon the use of flat patterns and clear contrasting colours was to have a great influence on designers of the second half of the nineteenth century.*

*Four dressers, published in N X Willemin,* Monuments français *(1806–39). This Gothic furniture was culled from fifteenth-century French and Flemish manuscripts, which also served as an important source for A W N Pugin. A variety of carved Gothic dressers arranged 'en buffet' with plate has been given special emphasis in this collection of designs. Their traceried ornamentation and canopied silhouettes appear in Pugin's* Gothic Furniture in the Style of the Fifteenth Century, *1835. Henry Shaw, in* Specimens of Ancient Furniture, *illustrated the dresser on the left in 1836.*

seat furniture. By 1835 his ideas on the design of Gothic furniture resulted in the publication of the first of his highly-influential series of books on Gothic design. This was entitled *Gothic Furniture in the Style of the Fifteenth Century*, and a number of the designs he published in this book were actually made for his commissions, beginning in 1837 with Scarisbrick Hall in Lancashire, his most important early commission.

Pugin's patron was Charles Scarisbrick, one of the many Catholic patrons who turned to him after his much-publicized conversion to the Roman Catholic Church in 1834. As Pugin pursued his antiquarian studies of Gothic architecture in Britain during the late 1820s and early 1830s, he became disgusted with the treatment of medieval buildings by the Church of England and came to the conclusion that Roman Catholics, who had represented the 'true Christians' of the Middle Ages,

would have cared for this medieval architectural heritage much better. For Pugin, an appreciation of Gothic architecture was indissoluble from belief in the religion of the Gothic age.

Pugin's outspoken conversion to Catholicism and criticism of the Anglican Church aroused great controversy in the 1830s, when full legal rights for Catholics had only recently been established. In 1836 Pugin published *Contrasts; or a Parallel Between the Noble Edifices of the Fourteenth and Fifteenth Centuries and Similar Buildings of the Present Day*, in which he lamented the 'degraded' state to which architectural design had sunk and suggested that the excellence of Gothic architecture was a product of the religious faith of architects during the Middle Ages. Such controversial views were not received warmly, and a witty Irishman named Mr McCann wrote the following poem, which found its way into the influential magazine the *Builder*:

*Oh have you seen the work just out,*
*By Pugin, the great builder?*
*'Architectural Contrasts' he's made out*
*Poor Protestants to bewilder.*
*The Catholic Church, she never knew –*
*Till Mr Pugin taught her,*
*That orthodoxy had to do*
*At all with bricks and mortar.*

*But now it's clear to one and all,*
*Since he's published his lecture,*
*No church is Catholic at all*
*Without Gothic architecture…*

The poem continued in a similar vein, poking fun at Pugin's earnest assertion that architectural design had declined steadily since the Reformation.

The early 1830s were a tumultuous time for Pugin. He married in 1831. The following year his young wife died in childbirth leaving him a baby daughter. His father died in 1832, followed by his mother in 1833, in which year he remarried. His conversion to Catholicism came in 1834, and Ferrey hints that it was the death of his staunchly Protestant mother which, although greatly affecting him, allowed him to convert in that year. Pugin initially settled in Salisbury, selecting the site because of the proximity of the great Gothic cathedral and other medieval monuments. He built a Gothic style house for himself and his family called St Marie's Grange which still stands today in somewhat modified form.

The style of Pugin's house was meant to be that of the fifteenth century, which he so admired. It was executed in brick in a boldly asymmetrical plan without a central hall, which must have made it somewhat inconvenient for all but a very small family. On the exterior were varied shapes of Gothic windows, sharply pointed roofs, and a small bell tower to one side of the house. Even Pugin's sympathetic friend and biographer, Benjamin Ferrey, described it as 'quaint and odd', showing the 'eccentricity of its owner'. Nonetheless, the house pleased Pugin and must have presented a striking contrast to the standard picturesque Gothic villa of the day. Ferrey tells us that Pugin was frequently at home in his fifteenth-century style Grange, 'collecting old books, prints, manuscripts, pictures, etc.' His collection of Gothic art was to become very extensive during the course of his career, and he frequently travelled to France and Belgium in order to make purchases. His antiquarian objects must have dominated the interior of his house.

Pugin's growing family and his increasing need to travel as his architectural practice expanded necessitated a move from Salisbury in 1841. Eventually he settled in Ramsgate in Kent, where he could keep a boat for forays to the Continent and where he was within easier reach of London. His new house, of larger scale, was named simply 'The Grange', and it was built in 1843 of the typical local materials: flint and stone. Beside The Grange, Pugin designed and built a beautiful private chapel dedicated to St Augustine with a richly decorated interior featuring stained glass and tiles made according to revived medieval techniques. The Grange and chapel, like his earlier house, still stand.

Just how did Pugin's Gothic designs of his adult career differ from the work of his contemporaries? The Gothic furniture he

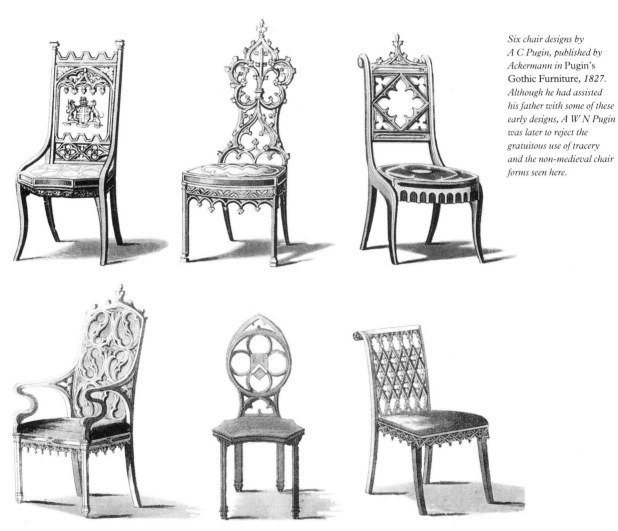

*Six chair designs by A C Pugin, published by Ackermann in* Pugin's Gothic Furniture, *1827. Although he had assisted his father with some of these early designs, A W N Pugin was later to reject the gratuitous use of tracery and the non-medieval chair forms seen here.*

designed for Windsor was typical of medievalism during the Regency period when tracery and other ornamental features from medieval ecclesiastical sources would be added to otherwise conventional domestic forms. This was an approach to Gothic design found since the eighteenth century with the furniture at Strawberry Hill, as hardly any examples of medieval furniture were then known. In his *Gothic Furniture* of 1835, Pugin began to publish furniture

designs based upon medieval types he had uncovered in the course of his antiquarian studies.

In Flemish interior scenes painted during the fifteenth century Pugin observed joined, box-like furniture with simple carved ornament and large metal handles and hinges. A tall side cabinet with a canopied top was based upon such Flemish examples and included in his book. One of his most influential designs was for an X-frame chair

*Opposite: Floor tiles by Herbert Minton to the designs of A W N Pugin, at the Church of St Augustine, Ramsgate, Kent, built by Pugin. The tiles are an example of the rich decoration executed by his loyal team of Crace, Minton, Hardman and Myers.*

*The Church of St Augustine and The Grange, Ramsgate, Kent, 1843 or 1844, shown in a lithograph by O Jewitt. Using the traditional local building materials of flint and stone, Pugin built a house (left) for himself and his large family at Ramsgate, where he kept a boat for journeys to the Continent. Next door to The Grange was his richly decorated private church dedicated to St Augustine.*

with armrests closely based upon examples he had observed in illuminated manuscripts. Such a chair appears with regularity in fifteenth-century manuscripts where a king or important personage sits enthroned on a X-frame chair under a canopy. Pugin observed that the medieval furniture he had seen in Britain and on the Continent was made of oak. It is possible that medieval furniture made of softer, less durable timbers simply did not survive. Pugin, however, concluded that oak was the only appropriate wood for Gothic style furniture. His first X-frame chair, made of oak, was produced in 1837 for Scarisbrick Hall.

The late medieval house at Scarisbrick had been encased in a stone façade of Gothic design during the Regency period. In the 1830s the eccentric bachelor Charles Scarisbrick, who was exceedingly wealthy, commissioned Pugin to remodel his family seat into something more convincingly

Gothic as a fitting repository for his considerable collection of art and antiquities. In the lavishly decorated Oak Room of the house, Pugin incorporated a number of Scarisbrick's carved Flemish panels and decorative elements dating from the fifteenth to the seventeenth centuries. The richly carved Red Drawing Room also continues the Flemish fifteenth-century theme that was so characteristic of Pugin's work during the 1830s. Any house with pretensions to medievalism had to have a Great Hall, and Pugin provided Charles Scarisbrick with an impressive one. This had the traditional elements of the late Middle Ages, such as an elaborately timbered ceiling decorated with simple stencilled designs and a carved tripart screen at one end.

The original exterior by Pugin featured a clock tower in which many observers have noted a likeness to the clock tower in the New Palace of Westminster that houses the

A detail of woodwork at Scarisbrick Hall, Lancashire, c1838. Apart from his youthful designs for George IV at Windsor, Scarisbrick was A W N Pugin's first major commission. The elaborate carving in oak and the profusion of naturalistic details are typical of his work during the 1830s.

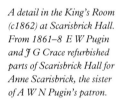

A detail in the King's Room (c1862) at Scarisbrick Hall. From 1861–8 E W Pugin and J G Crace refurbished parts of Scarisbrick Hall for Anne Scarisbrick, the sister of A W N Pugin's patron.

A detail in the King's Room (c1862) at Scarisbrick Hall. The theme of the room is the Kings and Queens of England.

The ceiling in The Great Hall at Scarisbrick. Pugin favoured the presence of the Great Hall in his grander domestic commissions, complete with a lantern for smoke and a Minstrels' Gallery. This fine, timbered ceiling, with its inverted V-shaped or cruck construction, was adapted from late medieval sources and covered with Pugin's richly coloured, stencilled designs.

famous bell known as 'Big Ben'. Pugin's Westminster design is known to have been inspired by his study of a well-known late medieval example in the town of Ypres in Belgium. At the time of the work at Scarisbrick, he would have just finished assisting Charles Barry with designs for the more ornamental details of the exterior at Westminster. The similarity between the two commissions is therefore not surprising.

Unfortunately the successor to the famous Westminster tower at Scarisbrick no longer exists, as Pugin's son, Edward Welby Pugin, replaced it with a much taller tower during his alterations to the house in the 1860s.

The mature phase of Pugin's career opened with the publication, in 1841, of his most important book, *The True Principles of Pointed or Christian Architecture*. This was nothing less than the manifesto in which he

*Design for a Marquetry Table Top by A W N Pugin, 1850. This beautiful design was sent to J G Crace's premises on Wigmore Street, London, where it was used for a large octagonal table with an oak base and marquetry top. The table was displayed in the Medieval Court of the 1851 Exhibition, where both Pugin and Crace received critical acclaim. In 1853 Crace supplied a virtually identical table for the owner of Abney Hall near Manchester; this later table is now in the Victoria & Albert Museum, London.*

linked spiritual belief to the quality of design, claiming that this connection between spirituality and art had produced artistic brilliance during the Gothic period. The frontispiece of the book illustrates a recognizable portrait of Pugin seated at his carved and traceried architect's desk designing with a compass, according to medieval practice. Around him are displayed medieval objects he had collected such as tiles, manuscripts, reliquaries, and architectural elements such as sections of colonettes he would have acquired in the course of his work. In the frontispiece Pugin wears his version of medieval dress with a loose, floppy head-dress and flowing robes. In real life, Ferrey tells us, Pugin's dress alternated between the nautical and the monastic.

Pugin went far beyond any previous practitioner of the Gothic Revival by advocating that the Gothic was the *only* architectural style, on both moral and practical grounds. In *The True Principles* he noted that in the Middle Ages, two-dimensional pattern, rather than three-dimensional perspective, was the basis for design. He concluded that flat decorative items such as textiles, carpets and wallpapers should likewise be designed in two-dimensional patterns with no shading to suggest perspective or depth. He dismissed the idea of designing a carpet in the manner of Gothic vaulting within an illusionistic architectural space, as a carpet was a flat surface on which to walk. To suggest otherwise was worse than illogical; it was positively dishonest in terms of design. This is a highly significant idea in the history of Western art, as it represents a turning

*An illustration published in A W N Pugin's* The True Principles, *1841. This plate illustrates the illusionism of design that Pugin felt was ridiculous, with its suggested vaulted niches looking onto garden fountains. If a surface were flat, Pugin felt that it should be decorated as such.*

away from the whole system of pictorial perspective re-discovered during the Renaissance. By rejecting this tradition in favour of the use of flat pattern, Pugin helped to promote the development of abstraction that was to become so characteristic of twentieth-century art and design.

Pugin, in common with his contemporaries, advocated the use of forms derived from nature as the proper basis for design. However, Pugin's doctrine of naturalism was that natural forms be used in a simplified and stylized fashion – that is, flattened and outlined in broad areas of colour, with no shading or perspectival effects. Some of the most beautiful designs of any nineteenth-century pattern book were those published in Pugin's next-to-last book, *Floriated Ornament* of 1849. This illustrated stylized leaf and flower designs in deep primary colours with white, chocolate brown, green and gilt. Such designs complemented the heraldic motifs that were stencilled onto

the architectural mouldings and ceilings of Pugin's interiors.

Apart from Pugin's role as the champion of flat pattern in design, his *True Principles* contained a most extraordinary and important statement, namely, that there should be 'no features about a building which are not necessary for convenience, construction or propriety.' The first two of these criteria for design were not, in fact, original to Pugin, but he made them famous by giving such emphasis to the importance of function in architecture and by claiming that only in the Gothic style was its ornamental vocabulary entirely functional. For example, he observed that the weight of a pinnacle in a Gothic building helped to pin down the buttresses, thereby stabilizing the vaulting.

Pugin also published a plate illustrating the 'false principles' of design, whereby ornament was used without thought for its purpose or suitability. In this illustration he

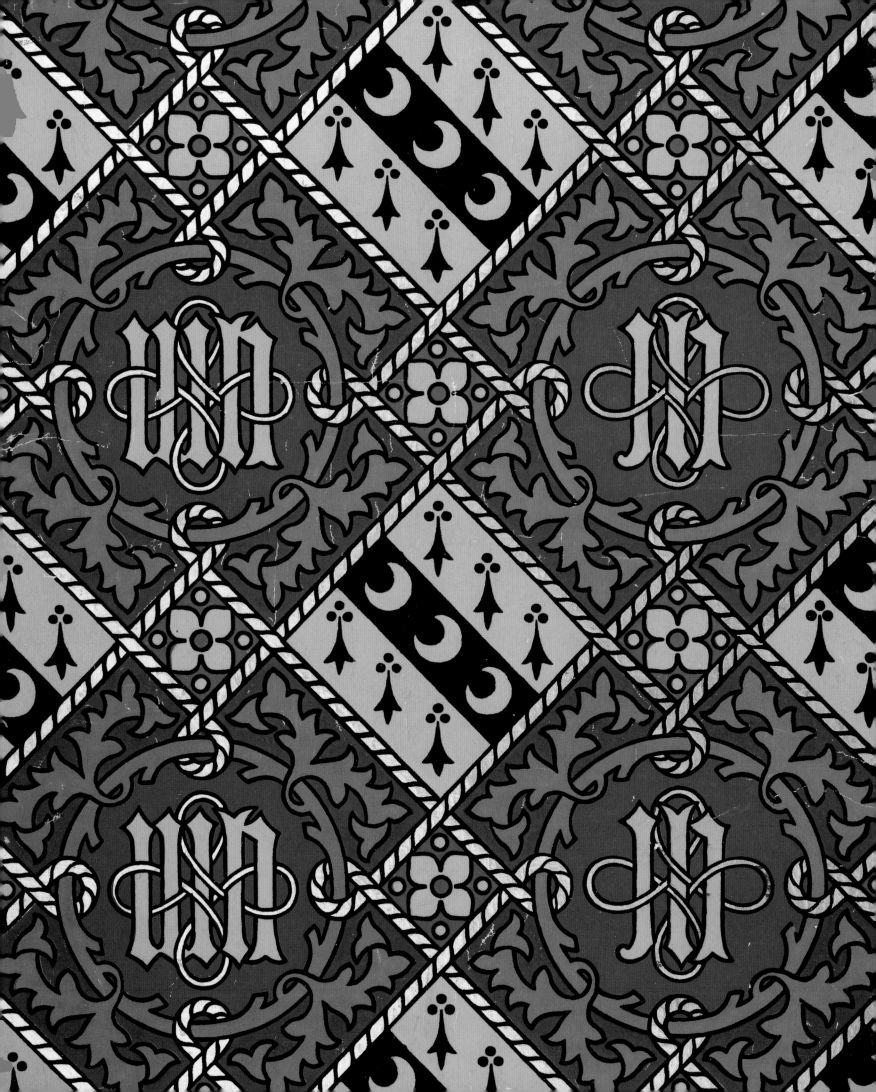

*A sample colourway for a wallpaper by A W N Pugin, designed for the Palace of Westminster in 1847. It was produced by J G Crace and features a stylized pomegranate pattern taken from Italian textiles of the late medieval period.*

*Opposite: A sample colourway for a wallpaper by A W N Pugin, c1845–50. In this design, ropes have been used to form a diaper pattern filled with monograms and heraldic elements. This is typical of Pugin's interest in patterned effects.*

*Design for a carpet, 1848, A W N Pugin. One of a group that Pugin sent to Crace for their decorating partnership, this carpet design was reproduced in 1976 for the Palace of Westminster.*

showed what he considered to be a very badly designed Gothic-style interior, saying he had 'perpetrated some of these enormities' himself at Windsor early in his career. He poked fun at the decorative use of vaulting derived from monuments like the Chapel of Henry VII at Westminster Abbey, a source used by Gothic Revivalists from Walpole to Wyatt. Pugin maintained that the imitation of a stone vault which, although decorative, actually had the function of holding up the roof, in papier mâché or other such 'sham' material was false design and 'dishonest', as such a feature pretended to be something it was not. Thus Pugin was opposed in principle to the illusionistic decorative techniques so prevalent in the Victorian era. Veneering over one wood with another, or painting plaster to look like marble, was as dishonest as pretending one had early sixteenth-century stone vaulting in one's sitting room.

Aside from the criteria of convenience and construction, however, Pugin had a third criterion for good design, and this was 'propriety'. Unlike the two ideas above, for which Pugin has sometimes been assigned a proto-modern role as a designer, the concept of propriety is a thoroughly nineteenth-century one that addresses the appropriateness of a given design to its context. In his plate illustrating the false principles of design, Pugin likened the application of ecclesiastical tracery and ornament in domestic interiors to a quotation out of context that did not respect its source.

An illustration of Pugin's notion of propriety in design can be seen in his correspondence with the Earl of Shrewsbury, one of his most important patrons and a leading Catholic aristocrat of his day. In a letter of 1841, Pugin wrote about the proposed designs for interiors at Alton Towers, Staffordshire, the dramatic battlemented seat of Lord Shrewsbury that was begun in 1810. Regarding the dining room, Pugin refused to work for the Earl unless he was allowed to 'make use of my knowledge and experience'

*Illustrations published in A W N Pugin's* Floriated Ornament, *1849. Pugin advocated the use of natural forms as the basis for ornamental design, but he stressed that these forms should be presented in a stylized, two-dimensional way, without shadows or illustrating perspective. He referred to the manuscripts and herbal treatises of the Middle Ages, examples of which he actually owned.*

*Two illustrations from
James K Colling's* Gothic
Ornaments, *vol. II, 1847,
showing polychromatic
details taken from
St Edmund's Chapel,
Westminster Abbey.
Colling became interested
in polychromy through the
studies of medieval churches
in Norfolk.*

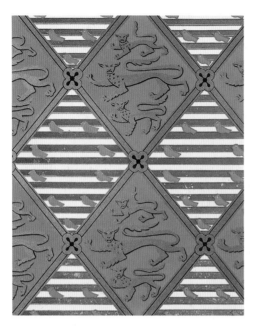

in the Gothic style. He would not proceed with the interior 'unless your lordship will consent to its being made worthy of your dignity and residence.' To Pugin, an interior that was 'unworthy' of the rank and status of his patron lacked propriety. Of equal impropriety was the window of the Alton Towers Dining Room, as it was 'a church window in design':

*From the first moment I spoke of a screen, and it is indispensable to break the current of air into the room. I never proposed anything for mere effect … and as regards the hall, I have nailed my colours to the mast, – a bay window, high open roof, lantern, two good fire-places, a great sideboard, screen, minstrel-gallery – all or none.*

It is difficult to imagine James Wyatt, William Atkinson, or any other architect

before him taking such a position with a client, but this extract from one of Pugin's letters illustrates the passion for Gothic convenience, construction and propriety that drove his career. That passion was harnessed for the most important task of his life in 1844, when he resumed work for Charles Barry at the Palace of Westminster once the rebuilding was under way. Pugin became the designer in charge of the interiors of the Palace, which rank as one of the most brilliant accomplishments of the nineteenth century. He designed woodwork and furniture of carved oak, tiles and carpets for the floors, papers for those walls not covered by frescos of scenes from British history, stencilled decorations for ceilings and mouldings, and metalwork and light fittings, all in a rich, resplendent Gothic style of the fifteenth century.

Recognizing that the Palace had been

The title page of
James K Colling's Gothic
Ornaments, vol. II, 1847.
Colling's first book was
inspired by his study of
Gothic architecture in
Norfolk. He subsequently
published three other books
on Gothic ornamental
details in which the use of
leaf forms was emphasized.
Colling's interest in
polychromy paralleled that
of Pugin, although his
naturalistic forms were more
complex, with less reliance
upon simple repetitive
geometric motifs.

the residence of the medieval kings (it was Henry VIII who moved his residence to Whitehall), Pugin designed Perpendicular Gothic interiors which are overwhelmingly comfortable, even inviting, in appearance. The New Palace was the seat of government of the British Empire. However, rather than designing it in the manner of a government building, Pugin chose the model of a medieval monarch's residence. Quiet, intimate niches and seating were scattered throughout the corridors of the Palace. Noise was controlled by means of carpets and textiles, ceilings were generally low except for the great ceremonial chambers, and the character of the interior was surprisingly domestic. It is surely one of the greatest achievements of Pugin's career that the

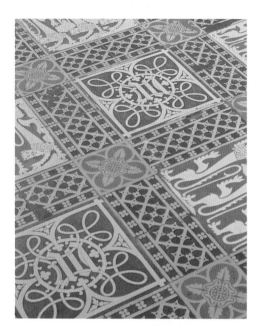

*The tiled floor of the Lords' Lobby at the Palace of Westminster, c1847. Herbert Minton's famous ceramics firm in Staffordshire supplied an enormous number of tiles, to A W N Pugin's designs, for the Palace of Westminster. The technique he revived for this was the lost medieval process of 'encaustic' tile-making, essentially a building-up of coloured layers of clay.*

*A detail of a brass door in the Lords' Chamber at the Palace of Westminster. John Hardman's metal-working firm in Birmingham supplied exquisite brass light fittings, door furniture and hardware, to Pugin's designs, for the Palace. Pugin used grillework in the form of Decorated Gothic tracery as part of the lavish interior scheme for the Lords' Chamber.*

*Opposite: The Royal Gallery in the Palace of Westminster, c1835–65. J G Crace assisted Pugin with the decoration of the Palace of Westminster interiors. The Royal Gallery functioned as a long, cere- monial interior traversed by the sovereign en route to the canopied throne in the Lords' Chamber. The wallpaper is one of a group Pugin designed after Italian textiles of the fifteenth and sixteenth centuries. The coloured stencilling of the architectural fittings and timbered ceiling, carried out by Crace's design firm, created a bold effect of abstraction.*

new parliamentary buildings on which he so decidedly stamped his character display his three criteria of good design: convenience, sound construction and propriety.

The Chamber of the House of Lords was opened in 1847. This was before the completion of the Commons as, in the nineteenth century, the Lords' Chamber was the more important of the two. The interior scheme stressed the medieval origins of the parliamentary system, with bronze statues of the barons who forced King John to sign the Magna Carta positioned around the room. Each statue was supported by angels that Pugin modelled after those in the magnifi- cent timbered roof of c1399 of Westminster Hall, which had survived the fire. Beneath a richly coloured timbered ceiling stencilled with heraldic motifs, Pugin designed a three- part throne raised on a dais in the medieval manner, covered by an ornately carved and

gilded canopy. This is still used today for the State Opening of Parliament. Stained glass, glittering light fittings of brass, finely carved panelling and woodwork, and seating for over 500 people completed the dazzling Lords' Chamber. It was to become one of the most influential interiors of the day. The American author Nathaniel Hawthorne pronounced it 'gravely gorgeous', and its decoration was re-cast for a group of country houses designed by Pugin towards the end of his life.

At Westminster, Pugin assembled a team of craftsmen and manufacturers upon whom he could rely to transform his hundreds of sketches into executed designs. For the revival of encaustic tiles in the medieval manner, Herbert Minton, heir to the famous ceramics factory in Staffordshire, was employed. John Hardman's family firm in Birmingham made exquisite metalwork

*The State Drawing Room at Knebworth House, Hertfordshire, 1844. The antiquary and historical novelist Sir Edward Bulwer-Lytton inherited the late medieval house of Knebworth in 1843. J G Crace, who had decorated Bulwer-Lytton's London townhouse, was employed in 1844 to decorate the principal rooms in the Gothic style, working in conjunction with a genealogist who researched the family lineage and coats of arms. The ceiling design, with its cusped and ogeed forms, represents Crace's own distinct brand of Gothic, while the design of the frieze has affinities with designs by Pugin, with whom Crace established a decorating business in 1844. Seen at the far right is a Gothic side table designed by Crace for the room.*

objects to Pugin's designs, while the builder George Myers carried out a great deal of work, even executing Gothic furniture on occasion. The man closest to Pugin was John Gregory Crace, the head of a well-established decorating firm founded in the 1760s. By 1844 Pugin and Crace had actually formed a partnership to decorate country houses in the Gothic style. One of their best-known collaborations was Eastnor Castle in Herefordshire, designed by Robert Smirke. Like Alton Towers (where the two men had worked separately and then together), Eastnor was a Regency castle with

*John Hardman of Birmingham made the brass door furniture for the Drawing Room at Eastnor Castle, Herefordshire, in 1850, to designs by A W N Pugin.*

*Opposite: The Drawing Room at Eastnor Castle, Herefordshire, 1849–50. A W N Pugin did not actually visit Eastnor Castle until the summer of 1850, when the work had almost been completed by J G Crace and his team. He praised Crace's painting of the early nineteenth-century ceiling, with its plaster pendants and fan vaulting, as well as the magnificent brass chandeliers executed by John Hardman to his designs. Crace's execution of the chimneypiece, with its sumptuous family tree of the Earl Somers, pleased him less.*

*This carved oak and marquetry work table at Eastnor Castle was presented to the third Countess Somers as a wedding present. It was designed by A W N Pugin and made by J G Crace in 1850. The trestle form and prominent drawer pulls were features Pugin had observed in furniture in fifteenth-century paintings and manuscripts. The quality of the workmanship is superb.*

a highly picturesque site. From 1849 to 1850 Pugin and Crace redecorated a Gothic Drawing Room and made furniture for Earl Somers, including an elaborately modelled, painted and gilded family tree for the Earl above the fireplace. The furniture, in oak with a rich walnut veneer and coloured marquetry, seems a bit surprising for the author of *The True Principles*, but it is in keeping with Crace's taste for rich effects. The Eastnor Drawing Room remains intact and can be seen today in all its splendour.

Pugin's final great work, and one which may have hastened his end, was preparing with his colleagues the Medieval Court for the Great Exhibition of 1851, held in the famous Crystal Palace in Hyde Park, London. Tens of thousands of visitors from around the world attended the exhibition, and Pugin knew this would be a good venue for advertising the Gothic decorative art he was designing. His team, Crace, Hardman, Minton and Myers all assisted him. The *Art Journal Illustrated Catalogue* referred to the 'large variety of those quaint and beautiful

works, designed by Mr Pugin.' As regards furniture, the *Journal* reported that:

*The furniture of the Medieval Court forms one of the most striking portions of the Exhibition, and has attracted a large amount of attention. The design and superintendence of these articles are by Mr Pugin, an artist who has studied the leading principles of medieval composition, and ornamental design, until his works are identified whenever they are seen. He has been ably seconded by Mr Crace, who has executed his designs. The two specimens on this page are their joint productions. The* Prie-Dieu *is very elegant, and is enriched with painting and gilding. The Cabinet is of oak, richly carved, and is decorated with characteristic brass-work of exceedingly bold design.*

George Myers also received praise for carving in wood and stone, along with Herbert Minton and John Hardman.

It is interesting to note that one critic of the day, Ralph Nicholson Wornum, suggested that the team were simply copying past

*A colour lithograph by Joseph Nash of The Medieval Court of the Great Exhibition, 1851. While some critics found the wares displayed at the Court rather too ecclesiastical in character, most were full of praise. A W N Pugin organized the Court, assisted by his 'team' of Crace, Minton, Hardman and the builder George Myers. The Court did much to introduce to the public Pugin's lavish style of Gothic decorative art.*

designs without creating anything new. However, he acknowledged the beauty of a Gothic table by Crace and a mantelpiece by Myers, commenting, 'As individual designs … this court offers some very fine samples of Gothic.' What he queried was not the quality of the objects displayed by Pugin and his team in the Medieval Court, but the very concept of reviving old forms. The idea of deriving principles of design from the art of the past and creating a new, uniquely nineteenth-century style was to become of overwhelming importance to art critics in the second half of that century. Once the idea of interpreting the past became widespread, it was inevitable that the archaeological approach to Gothic design would fall from favour.

The Great Exhibition had taken place in May of 1851, when Pugin was involved in various commissions and continuing work for the Palace of Westminster. By February 1852 he had a breakdown in his health from which he never really recovered. Ferrey observed that 'his labours aged him prematurely.' During much of 1852 his mind was deranged, and in September he died, aged 40. The same year saw the death of A J Downing, who had done so much to promote the Gothic in America.

The recognition of Pugin's contribution to art and design was widespread and immediate. Queen Victoria, unprompted, granted his widow a pension from the Civil List. The critic Edmund Sheridan Purcell added an appendix to Ferrey's biography of

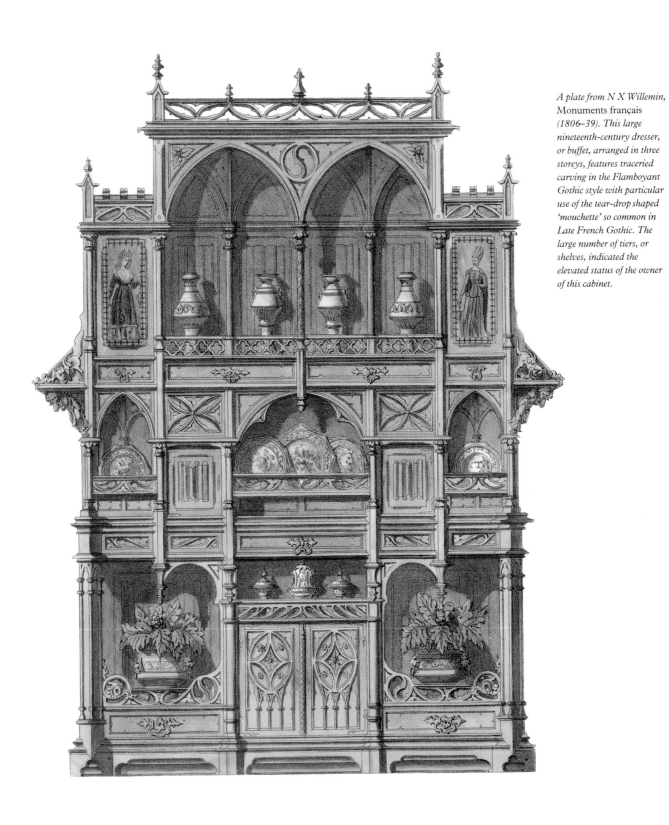

A plate from N X Willemin, Monuments français (1806–39). This large nineteenth-century dresser, or buffet, arranged in three storeys, features traceried carving in the Flamboyant Gothic style with particular use of the tear-drop shaped 'mouchette' so common in Late French Gothic. The large number of tiers, or shelves, indicated the elevated status of the owner of this cabinet.

*An illustration of medieval metalwork, published in M D Wyatt's* Metalwork and its Artistic Design, *1852. William Burges, later to become an architect of note, assisted Matthew Digby Wyatt in his scholarly publication on medieval metalwork. This illustration shows the type of objects that had directly inspired the metalwork designs of Pugin.*

*Design for a bookcase by*
*A W N Pugin, published in*
Gothic Furniture in the
Style of the Fifteenth
Century *(1835). The use of*
*rich Flamboyant Gothic*
*details here indicate Pugin's*
*affinity to French and*
*Flemish Gothic design.*

Pugin, begun in the mid-1850s, lamenting his untimely death:

*… for the light of his genius to be extinguished; for the rich treasures of his learning, gathered from ancient lore or from modern enlightenment, to be scattered and wasted, all the years of labour to be in vain – the ripe mind, the pure taste, the correct judgment – is indeed a loss, not to himself alone, but to mankind.*

Certainly, with the death of Pugin the Gothic Revival lost the greatest practitioner it has ever known, and some of the spirit and vigour of the Revival departed with him. Pugin's knowledge was not, however, 'scattered and wasted', as Purcell had feared. His ideas were to form the groundwork for a new emerging generation of designers in the second half of the nineteenth century.

*The Drawing Room at Tower House, Melbury Road, London, 1875–81. William Burges was an antiquarian architect and designer, and the themes found in his buildings and furniture are highly literary. Here the inspiration was the medieval epic,* The Romance of the Rose. *The sculptor Thomas Nicholls executed this and many other rich programmes of sculpture, which were central to Burges's three-dimensional, theatrical-type Gothic.*

My own feeling is, that, as in the pointed arch we have not only the most beautiful, but at the same time incomparably the most convenient feature in construction which has ever been, or which, I firmly believe, ever can be invented, we should not be true artists if we neglected to use it... it is at once the most beautiful and the most economical way of doing the work we have to be done. *G E Street*, Brick and Marble in the Middle Ages: Notes of a Tour in the North of Italy *(1855)*

The death of the great Gothic Revivalist Pugin in 1852 hastened public recognition of his remarkable achievements. Not long after his death an article in the *Times* offered the following endorsement of his 'true principles', while acknowledging the view of some of his critics:

*With all his crotchets, and with an absurd attachment, not merely to the spirit, but to the letter of medievalism, he has perhaps done more for architecture than any of those who run him down. He it was who first exposed the shams and concealments of modern architecture, and contrasted it with the heartiness and sincerity of medieval work. He showed the fair outside of a modern building, having no relation to its construction, except that of a screen to hide its clumsy makeshifts. He then showed how the first principle of medieval work was to expose construction, and not to hide it, but to adorn it. A modern building, for example, conceals its flying buttresses with a dead wall; an ancient one exposes them and derives a principal charm from these contrivances being seen. It is the law of all the old architecture – there is nothing which it fears to show; it rather invites inspection within and without; whereas concealment was for long the rule of modern British architecture – concealment of the real material – concealment of the manner of construction. Pugin is dead – died, we believe, in distress. Let us remember to his honour that, if now there seems to be the dawn of a better architecture, if our edifices seem to be more correct in taste, more genuine in material, more honest in construction, and more sure to last, it was he who first showed us that our architecture offended not only against the laws of beauty, but also against the laws of morality.*

After Pugin's death a circle of his friends, admirers, and his eldest son continued to design in a Gothic Revival style close to his. One of the post-Pugin generations of Gothic Revivalists was George Gilbert Scott, the man who wrote that he was 'awakened from my slumber by the thunder of Pugin's writings.' Scott, the author of *Gothic Architecture, Secular and Domestic* of 1857, was the son of a clergyman and became deeply involved with the reform of church architecture and ritual that was of great concern to the Anglican Church during the middle of the nineteenth century. The Ecclesiology Movement developed in two distinct camps centred around the medieval university towns of Oxford and Cambridge. Pugin himself had contributed to the debate about 'proper' church architecture with a book on the importance of rood screens towards the end of his life. However, the fervour with which the Victorians debated such ecclesiological points is hard to comprehend within the very secular context of the twentieth century. Instead, Scott is best remembered today as the architect of the imposing Midland Hotel at St Pancras Station and the Albert Memorial in Kensington Gardens in London. Both structures date from the 1860s and display the rich, Anglo-French, Decorated Gothic style that typifies Scott's work.

George Gilbert Scott represented the more conservative followers of Pugin, as did John Gregory Crace, the decorator with whom Pugin had worked closely for eight years. Scott and Crace collaborated in the architecture and furnishing of a Gothic house very much influenced by the ideas of Pugin. This was Pippbrook House in

Two doorcases in Windsor, Berkshire, mid-nineteenth century. Builders adapted the Gothic style to modest domestic architecture most readily in towns where medieval monuments already existed, as was the case in Windsor.

Two doorcases in Reading, Berkshire (left) and Ludlow, Shropshire (right), of the later nineteenth century. These doorcases, with their brick arches, naturalistic details and patterned brick-work, show the influence of John Ruskin's ideas.

*A carpet from Scarisbrick Hall, Lancashire, c1862. At the time of A W N Pugin's death in 1852, J G Crace had hundreds of Pugin's designs for decorative art in his premises in London. Throughout the 1850s and 60s Crace reinterpreted these ideas, as seen here in what is certainly the finest surviving carpet of the Gothic Revival.*

*The stables, Scarisbrick Hall, Lancashire, 1861–8. E W Pugin's influence was primarily from Late Gothic architecture on the Continent. With its low, conical tower, the stable block is distinct from the architecture of the house.*

Dorking, Surrey, built in 1856 to Scott's designs and furnished by J G Crace, who can be said to have interpreted, rather than followed to the letter, the designs of Pugin. Crace, in conjunction with the old team of Minton and Hardman, was able to continue to use the large number of Pugin's designs that remained in the Crace firm's premises in Wigmore Street, London. These designs were later divided between the Royal Institute of British Architects and the Victoria and Albert Museum in London by Crace's son, who was to remind the public of the achievements of Pugin through an article published in 1894 in the *Journal of the Royal Institute of British Architects*.

During the 1850s Crace continued to work in the Pugin manner for a small group of country house commissions they had undertaken together shortly before Pugin's death. These included Abney Hall in Cheadle, near Manchester; Leighton Hall near Welshpool; and Lismore Castle in Co.

Waterford, Ireland. In these houses the inspiration of Pugin's ideas is very clear, yet there hardly exists a design for wall treatments, chimneypieces, or furniture that was copied exactly from Pugin's drawings and sketches. It is typical of the more conservative Gothic Revivalists such as Scott and Crace that, while acknowledging the importance of Pugin's ideas about 'sound construction', they nonetheless paid greater attention to the Gothic vocabulary of ornament he established. The *Times* article quoted above mentioned Pugin's exposing of construction in order to adorn it. This concern for Gothic decoration was to unite the work of the more conservative Gothic designers of the post-Pugin generation.

As J G Crace had been a close business associate and an admirer of Pugin, it is understandable that he should have continued to work on two of A W N Pugin's commissions, the Palace of Westminster and Scarisbrick Hall, with Pugin's eldest son, Edward Welby Pugin, who took over his father's practice at the age of 17. A passion-ate personality who shared his father's religious feelings, E W Pugin was also to die prematurely in a distressed state of mind. His work, most notably interiors such as the Queen's Robing Room in the Palace of Westminster, displays a complicated, rich style of Gothic which can be most closely compared with Flamboyant Gothic on the Continent. Indeed, E W Pugin was to receive commissions for two country houses in Belgium during the course of his career, indicating his close links with the Gothic Revival in Europe.

Charles Scarisbrick, the eccentric bachelor who had been the patron of

*Metalwork at Carlton Towers, Yorkshire, 1873–5. E W Pugin certainly relied upon the designs of his father and particularly on those designs published in* The True Principles *(1841). Nevertheless, these details of metalwork illustrate a greater interest in naturalism.*

*Opposite: Carlton Towers, Yorkshire, 1873–5. The ornamentation of this Entrance Porch in the Flamboyant Gothic style typifies the rich, continentally-inspired designs of E W Pugin. The owner, Lord Beaumont, had converted to Catholicism in 1869, and he advertised his medieval ancestry by 'Gothicizing' his Jacobean hall.*

A W N Pugin, died in 1860. As his children by his German mistress were illegitimate, his equally eccentric sister Anne, who soon styled herself 'Lady Scarisbrick', inherited Scarisbrick Hall and decided to alter it by adding a new east wing. The architect was Edward Welby Pugin. Crace decorated the interiors, assisted by Minton and Hardman. The younger Pugin added an enormous tower to the house, replacing his father's clock tower. The Continental flavour of E W Pugin's Gothic is best seen in the design of the Scarisbrick stables, which have turrets and conical towers in the manner of a chateau in the Loire Valley. The stable block was built in the late 1860s, and in its bold, three-dimensional forms and rather fanciful elements derived from medieval fortifications it is in tune with the work of other emerging Gothic Revival architects who stressed the story-book, fantasy element of the Gothic past. This approach to the Gothic was particularly used in France and Germany during the second half of the nineteenth century.

Edward Pugin continued the fantastical character of his Gothic design in his alterations of 1873–5 to a large country house, Carlton Towers in Yorkshire. The original house, Carlton Hall, dated to the Jacobean period and had received alterations in the eighteenth century. In 1869, when E W Pugin had just finished work at Scarisbrick, a new patron materialized in the shape of Henry Stapleton, who became the second Lord Beaumont by virtue of his family claim to a dormant medieval Barony. In 1869 Lord Beaumont came of age and converted to Catholicism, so the younger Pugin would have been much in sympathy with him. His new patron wished for a Barons' Hall, chapel, and keep for Carlton Towers, as his seat was now to be known. E W Pugin's designs for these were published in the *Building News* early in 1874, but they were never executed, owing to financial difficulties.

Instead, Pugin faced the entire existing building in a rather crisp, repetitive Gothic style with dripstone mouldings, battlements, and mullioned windows with Perpendicular tracery. Of more interest were the high clock tower, gargoyles and waterspouts, and the stair tower with spirally-placed windows in the manner of the famous example at Blois, which dates to the sixteenth century. The

*Plate LXVII from Owen Jones's* The Grammar of Ornament *(1856). This plate illustrates medieval ornament taken from illuminated manuscripts from the ninth to the fourteenth century. Jones's* Grammar *was a compilation of ornamental designs in a wide variety of styles intended as a source book for professional designers.*

stair tower at Carlton Towers and the enormous ogee arch and Flamboyant detailing of the Entrance Porch indicate once again the extent of E W Pugin's Continental influences. He did not live to complete more than the shell of Lord Beaumont's fantasy castle, however, and there is evidence to suggest that, had the younger Pugin not died of a heart attack at the age of 41, he might have been dismissed from Carlton Towers owing to his increasingly eccentric and belligerent behaviour.

In March of 1875 John Francis Bentley, later to become known as the architect of the Roman Catholic Cathedral of Westminster, began to prepare designs for the interiors at Carlton Towers. Bentley's career was essentially as an ecclesiastical architect, but Carlton Towers represents a very successful example of his domestic style. He decorated

and furnished the state apartments of the house in a richly ornamented Gothic. The most lavish interior was the Venetian Drawing Room, so-called because of the collection of Venetian glass displayed within it. Bentley spent much time selecting and designing wallpapers, stained glass, window furniture and other elements for his interiors, which gave them a character of great richness that can be likened to the Gothic interiors by A W N Pugin and J G Crace. Like them, Bentley used a team of skilled craftsmen, including the potter William de Morgan, who supplied the tiles for the fireplace of the Venetian Room. The iconography of the room was taken from Shakespeare's *The Merchant of Venice*, and scenes from the play were painted in panels by the artist N H J Westlake. As at Eastnor Castle, where Pugin and Crace had worked,

*Two details of 'Italian Brickwork' published by G E Street in* Brick and Marble in the Middle Ages *(1855). The details are taken from windows in Verona, which Street praised for their 'combined delicacy and richness of no common degree, so much does carefully-arranged and contrasted colour do for architecture.'*

the family heraldry was displayed above the chimneypiece. Bentley's Venetian Room at Carlton Towers certainly ranks as one of the more imaginative interiors of the later Gothic Revival, paralleling the breathtaking Gothic rooms created by William Burges.

E W Pugin, Crace, and Scott are representatives of one stream of design that flowed from the ideas of A W N Pugin. Their work is characterized by great richness and by an appreciation of the decorative vocabulary of Gothic ornament in the Perpendicular style that Pugin had established. Another stream of Gothic, which was to prove more original and innovative, was pursued by a group of designers who began to explore the use of polychromy, or colour, in architecture. This was one of the distinct contributions of the Gothic Revival to modern architecture.

Through his writings and his executed work, Pugin had done much to promote the application of boldly contrasting colours to the walls, ceilings, and architectural features of a room, yet the idea was not original to

him. In the 1820s a French architect named Jacques-Ignace Hittorf had published two important volumes: *Architecture Antique de la Sicile* and *Architecture Polychrome des Grecs*. Both these books put forth the astounding observation that traces of colour could be found on ancient sculpture and architecture. It was a great shock for those at the time to realize that most ancient monuments, from the Parthenon to Exeter Cathedral, had been painted in bright colours both inside and out. Followers of Pugin such as Scott and Crace began to use colour to a great extent in their designs. Pugin's use of stencilling designs to create layers of boldly-coloured pattern, paralleled in the work of his great contemporary, the French architect Eugène Viollet-le-Duc, was a direct result of antiquarian study of the art of the Middle Ages.

The 1850s saw the emergence of another type of polychromy – this time achieved by the use of varied and contrasting building materials, such as coloured brick and stone. A growing number of architects and designers began to look at medieval

*Details of polychromatic decoration designed by William Burges's, Cardiff Castle, Wales, c1868–85. The influence of the Hispano-Moresque tradition can be seen in Burges's work through his use of interlocking geometric forms such as stars and crosses.*

*Opposite: Polychromy at Cardiff Castle. Burges's colour contrasts frequently featured bluegreen and gold, an unusual combination for his day.*

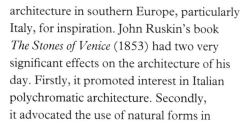

architecture in southern Europe, particularly Italy, for inspiration. John Ruskin's book *The Stones of Venice* (1853) had two very significant effects on the architecture of his day. Firstly, it promoted interest in Italian polychromatic architecture. Secondly, it advocated the use of natural forms in ornamentation. The quintessential 'Ruskinian' building in an Italianate Gothic was the Oxford University Museum, begun in 1855 by the Irish architects Thomas Deane and Benjamin Woodward, who had already built a polychromatic Venetian Gothic museum in Dublin at Trinity

*Two views of the exterior of All Saints Church, Margaret Street, London, by William Butterfield, 1849–59. The bold simplified shapes of Butterfield's designs allow them to make a powerful visual impression, as seen in the detail (right) of the iron railing.*

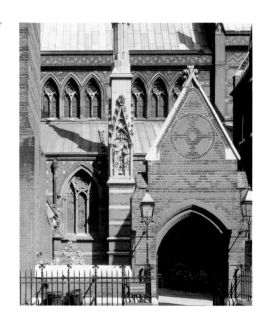

*Opposite: A view of the interior towards the altar, All Saints Church. The use of rich building materials to achieve an effect of polychromy was inspired by John Ruskins's* The Seven Lamps of Architecture *(1849).*

College. Two Irish brothers, the O'Sheas, carved the naturalistic stone details of leaves and flowers on the exterior of the Oxford Museum. Ruskin was very interested in this ornamentation, and one of the window designs has been attributed to him. The first major monument of the new polychromatic Gothic architecture of the 1850s, which was actually designed before the publication of Ruskin's important book, was All Saints Church in London by the architect William Butterfield. The eldest son of the large family of a London chemist, Butterfield served his apprenticeship with a builder in London and then worked several years in architects' offices before setting up his own practice in 1840 as a Gothic Revival architect. He was a dedicated Ecclesiologist and a member of the High Church Movement. He was particularly interested in designing proper ecclesiastical fittings. The vast majority of his executed buildings were

churches, including the Anglican Cathedrals of Adelaide and Melbourne in Australia and Fredericton in New Brunswick, Canada.

The site of All Saints, in Margaret Street in the West End of London, was cramped and narrow, yet Butterfield succeeded in giving the parish a church which not only appears spacious from the inside, but which is characterized by a striking richness of design. The architectural historian Sir John Summerson, who almost single-handedly resuscitated Butterfield's reputation earlier in this century, commented on the 'startling' use of red and black bricks to form bands and diapering in All Saints, for at this date 'true Gothic men clung to stone.' Butterfield looked to earlier Gothic models than had Pugin, for he considered the Perpendicular style of the fifteenth century to be the debased, over-refined phase of the Gothic. Instead, in common with a whole generation of post-

*All Saints Church, Margaret Street, London, 1849–59. This detail of the baptismal font shows the stump columns and polychromy that are a trademark of Butterfield's Gothic.*

*All Saints Church. Butterfield's simple, stylized leaf forms in light alabaster, contrasting with darker granite colonettes, strongly recall the classic early English nave piers and capitals at Salisbury Cathedral. Butterfield was part of a generation of Gothic Revivalists who looked to early Gothic forms for inspiration. George Myers, who worked closely with A W N Pugin, carved the capitals.*

Pugin architects, he looked to the Gothic of the thirteenth and fourteenth centuries, the Early English and Decorated Gothic, according to Rickman's terminology.

Part of the boldness of his architecture is no doubt due to the fact that, instead of piercing his walls with large traceried windows, a typical feature of the Perpendicular style, Butterfield used considerable areas of unbroken wall in his designs. The interior of All Saints is striking in the polychromatic effect created by the use of coloured marble and stone. Summerson has suggested that Butterfield travelled to Siena; certainly the church is reminiscent of the Sienese Gothic.

The parsonage, vicarage or rectory was normally the province of the architect who designed its associated church. Many ecclesiological architects consequently designed domestic architecture principally in this context. The few houses designed by Butterfield are of great architectural interest

and charm. For example, the modest, five-bedroomed parsonage at Great Woolstone in Buckinghamshire, begun in 1851, has a gabled brick exterior remarkably free of decorative details, except for a few recessed pointed arches in brickwork above the principal windows. These are varied in size but neither traceried nor of stone, having many small panes and being painted in white. The house anticipates to a great degree the Red House that Philip Webb was to build eight years later.

Aside from William Butterfield, the major force in polychromatic Gothic of the 1850s and 60s was the architect George Edmund Street. Indeed, it might fairly be said that Street's office nurtured the next generation of Gothic Revivalists. G E Street had been a pupil of Scott and, like him, was deeply involved with church architecture during his career. One of his most pleasing small churches was that at Toddington, in

*A detail of the richly coloured stonework in All Saints Church. Butterfield was inspired by Italian medieval churches in his work here.*

Gloucestershire, built to contain the tombs of Charles Hanbury Tracy, the amateur architect of Toddington, and his wife. Street's best-known building today is the Law Courts in London, designed in the 1860s in his richly ornamented polychromatic Gothic, but not actually finished until nearly 20 years later. Street was the winner of the competition to design this important public building in 1866, by which time Gothic had become an accepted style for civic and institutional architecture.

*Opposite: The Royal Law Courts, London, designed in 1868 by G E Street. A pupil of Scott, Street trained a number of important designers in his office. By the 1860s the Gothic had become an acceptable style for public and civic architecture. Street's repeated use of capped conical turrets and repetitive, sharply pointed arcades indicates the extent of his interest in Continental Gothic architecture.*

*A detail of the entrance of the Natural History Museum, London, 1873–86. Here the architect Alfred Waterhouse mixed Romanesque elements, notably the large round arched tympanum above the entrance, with the Gothic, as seen in the variety of leaf capitals. Polychromy and the contrast of textures achieved with modelled terracotta details are the hallmarks of Waterhouse's style.*

In choosing models, Street began to look further afield than Pugin or Scott had done for inspiration. He made the usual pilgrimages to France and Germany, but he also studied and published the medieval architecture of Italy and Spain, which displayed the abstraction of Early Christian and Islamic design and which used more colourful building materials such as coloured marble and brick in addition to light-coloured stone. The use of building materials to produce such a vivid contrast of colours and textures was a revelation to Gothic Revival architects in the 1850s. Immediately a fresh appearance was given to Gothic buildings by means of more purely geometric ornamental forms, the bold massing of silhouettes, and the use of coloured brick for pattern on exteriors.

Robert Kerr, who published a middle-class manual of taste entitled *The Gentleman's House: or, how to plan English residences from the parsonage to the palace* in 1864, observed that 'There is a spirited and substantial vigour in the presently prevailing revival of medieval architecture.' He added, 'People may not sympathize with the demands of Pre-Raphaelite enthusiasm… they may very fairly be permitted to express a doubt whether so singular an enthusiasm as this 'Gothic mania' ever seized upon Art before, or ever will seize upon it again.'

*The tower of Salamanca
Cathedral, Spain,
published in G E Street's*
Some Account of Gothic
Architecture in Spain
*(1865). Street described
the tower as demonstrating
'that dignified manliness
of architectural character
which so very few of our
modern architects ever seem
even to strive for.'*

*The frontispiece to G E Street's* Brick and Marble in the Middle Ages *(1855). Here Street has chosen the north porch of Sta Maria Maggiore in Bergamo, Italy, in order to illustrate the varied geometric forms and use of contrasting building materials he admired in Italian medieval architecture.*

*A plate of the Campanile, S. Andrea, Mantua, Italy, published by G E Street in* Brick and Marble in the Middle Ages *(1855). Street criticized the 'awkward and abrupt manner in which the octagonal stage and the round tile spire are set upon the square tower.'*

However, concluded Kerr, there was no denying the 'muscularity' of this new version of the Gothic style.

Gothic churches, parsonages, schools, institutional buildings and mansion blocks with patterned brickwork and contrasting stone became familiar landmarks all over cities in England during the second half of the nineteenth century, particularly during the 1860s, 70s and 80s. Alfred Waterhouse's Museum of Natural History in South Kensington, begun in 1873, is one notable example of the genre that originated with architects like Street and Butterfield. Waterhouse began his practice in Manchester

*The exterior of the Natural History Museum, London, 1873–86. More than any other architect, Alfred Waterhouse created a Gothic civic architecture with his designs for Manchester Assize Courts and Town Hall, Reading's Town Hall and the Natural History Museum in London, which rises boldly like a cathedral in the Rhine Valley. Waterhouse's massive, simple silhouettes were well suited to institutional architecture.*

*The Royal Albert Memorial, London, 1864–72. George Gilbert Scott was an established architect of the Gothic Revival by the time he was chosen to design the memorial in Kensington Gardens. It is based upon the shape of a medieval shrine. Shortly afterwards Scott designed the parish church of Kensington, not far away. Both buildings are highly competent (rather than exciting) essays in a 'High Gothic' style of about 1300.*

*Opposite: Holly Lodge, Highgate, London, 1865. Holly Village was designed by H A Darbishire to the commission of the philanthropist Baroness Burdett-Coutts on behalf of her servants. While owing something to Ruskin, the ornamental details of Darbishire's Gothic style also look to French and Flemish sources.*

in 1856 before setting up in London in 1865. In the 1870s he undertook the design of two gabled and richly ornamented town halls in polychromatic Gothic at Manchester and Reading, as well as rebuilding Porden's immense Eaton Hall in Cheshire for the Duke of Westminster (now demolished).

In the New World, similar examples of muscular polychromatic Gothic began to appear, chiefly due to the influence of Ruskin's writing. The little-known American architect P B Wight designed a number of public buildings in the New York area in the manner of medieval Venetian palazzi. The outstanding example was the National Academy of Design (now demolished), built between 1863 and 1865 on Fourth Avenue. For the interiors of his buildings, Wight designed beautifully coloured, patterned decorative schemes that can be traced

back to the publications of Pugin for their inspiration. In Canada, the Parliament complex in Ottawa was begun in 1861 in the muscular, polychromatic Gothic style inspired by Ruskin. The architect was Thomas Fuller, from Bath, who had arrived in Canada when Deane and Woodward's Oxford Museum was in progress. The Museum had a noticeable influence upon Fuller's designs for the Canadian Parliament buildings, which were rebuilt and enlarged after a fire in 1916.

'Ruskinian' Gothic was also seen in smaller buildings during the second half of the nineteenth century. The delightful Holly Village in Highgate was built in 1865 as housing for her servants by the philanthropist Baroness Burdett Coutts. The architect of the small group of Gothic cottages was the little-known H A Darbishire,

*Four details of brickwork from J Lacroux's,* La Brique Ordinaire *(1878). By 1860 the process of brick-making had become so industrialized as to make bricks widely available as an inexpensive building material. This, and the emphasis on exterior polychromy achieved in bricks by architects such as William Butterfield, led to the great popularity of ornamental brickwork during the second half of the nineteenth century.*

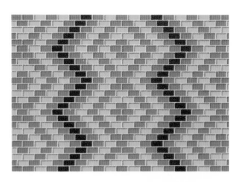
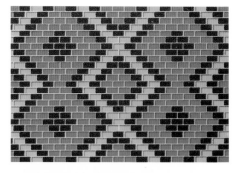
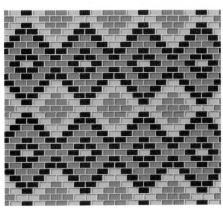
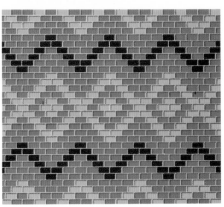

who built other blocks of housing for Baroness Coutts, as well as Columbia Market in Bethnal Green in the East End of London, inspired by the Flemish Gothic that Pugin had admired. Ruskin's poly-chromatic Gothic was used for almshouses and other 'social' architecture in many parts of Britain, where its Christian connotations were seen as appropriate.

Many Gothic gate lodges and estate cottages were built in the grounds of country houses during the nineteenth century. However, the Gothic style was rarely adopt-ed for modest town houses as the expense of recreating the style was often prohibitive. The architectural historian Henry Russell Hitchcock noted that George Gilbert Scott

built a little terrace of Gothic houses adjacent to Westminster Abbey in the middle of the nineteenth century. He continued, 'Scott's houses had little influence, however. Gothic terraces were no more popular in the fifties and sixties in England than in the preceding decades.' A further difficulty was that of finding workmen trained in the Gothic style. The notable exception to this was towns where there were major Gothic monuments such as Oxford and Salisbury, where both workmen and models for Gothic design were readily available.

There was, however, a more indirect but widespread influence of the Revival on ordinary terraced housing, largely through a popular understanding of the lectures and

*Plate 31, Design for a Villa, from J Lacroux's* La Brique Ordinaire *of 1878. Intended as a practical manual for builders, Lacroux's book showed a range of styles of architecture, with accompanying patterns of brickwork. Here he illustrates an impressive-looking villa with Gothic features suitable for a prosperous middle-class patron.*

writings of John Ruskin. The polychromy Ruskin so admired in Italian Gothic emerged in the hands of British builders as patterned brickwork, especially in layers of red and grey brick. Furthermore, the naturalism emphasized by Ruskin, and so meticulously observed by the O'Shea brothers in their details for the Oxford Museum, was to be translated by builders into stucco capitals with leaf decoration that can be seen on terraced houses throughout Britain.

A group of young architect-designers who trained in the office of G E Street was to shift the emphasis from archaeological medievalism to a more general sense of medieval form. Among them was Richard

*A pair of terraced houses in Bentham Road, Hackney, London, c1860. While most builders avoided the Gothic style, these houses in Hackney represent an unusual example of a Gothic terrace. During the mid-nineteenth century, this area of London was being developed rapidly by speculative building.*

*A house in North Oxford, c1870. Executed in the local stone of the region, the large areas of solid wall and simplified geometric forms of the design link this house to the 'muscular Gothic' of the 1860s and 70s.*

*The entrance porch of terraced houses, Hornsey, London, c1870. A simple Gothic porch was added to give architectural character to these terraced houses.*

*A vicarage in Camden, London, late nineteenth century. The coloured bands of brickwork seen here link the design to the ideas popularized by John Ruskin.*

*Opposite: The Entrance Lodge, Eaton Hall, Cheshire, 1870–83. The architect Alfred Waterhouse replaced Porden's Eaton Hall with a 'muscular Gothic' during the final quarter of the nineteenth century. This Eaton Hall was demolished in 1961, leaving the Entrance Lodge as a reminder of Waterhouse's most spectacular domestic commission.*

Norman Shaw, who became well-known as a designer of this new 'Reformed Gothic' furniture and decorative art at the International Exhibition of 1862 in London. The objects displayed by Reformed Gothic designers used bold, massive forms combined with colourful, often stylized ornament in an attempt to get back to 'real' medieval design of the thirteenth and fourteenth centuries. An emphasis was placed on handicraft rather than machine production; on patterned wallhangings of wool with embroidery rather than wallpapers printed in perspective designs; and on rich dark colours produced by means of traditional dyes rather than modern chemically-produced colours. Furniture and woodwork was designed to reveal its construction and was ornamented with simple carving.

Shaw, born in Edinburgh, became Street's principal assistant in 1859 and set up business in his own architectural practice

*An illustration of an interior, published in Bruce Talbert's* Examples of Ancient and Modern Furniture, *1876. The Scottish designer Talbert was responsible for spreading the message of 'Reformed Gothic' to a wider audience during the 1860s and 70s. The ornamental vocabulary he popularized included the use of shortened 'stump' columns, geometric panelling and chamfering, and polygonal cutting. Reformed Gothic can be viewed as a turning away from the literal use of Gothic forms towards a fresh interpretation of the style.*

*'An Interior View of a Library', by W Wilkinson, late nineteenth century. The ideas of Reformed Gothic designers such as Talbert are seen here. Typical features of the second half of the nineteenth century are to be found in the grid-like pattern of the writing desk panelling and the splayed legs of the accompanying chair, suggesting an affinity with later design movements such as the Aesthetic Movement and Art Nouveau.*

*An oak sideboard with inlay of ebony, walnut, box and holly, designed by Bruce Talbert and made by Holland and Sons of London, c1865. The early date of this sideboard ensures that it lacks the pronounced use of stump columns and chamfering typical of Talbert's mature work (see right). Nonetheless, the simple, box-like silhouette and restrained use of geometric ornament signal the Reformed Gothic style.*

*An illustration of a sideboard published in Bruce Talbert's* Examples of Ancient and Modern Furniture, *1876, showing Talbert's Reformed Gothic style.*

in 1862. In that year, in the International Exhibition, he showed a remarkable book-case cabinet of oak with polychromatic decoration in bold, geometric repeated patterns, with arcading, stump-like columns and exaggerated metalwork fittings very similar to those Pugin had illustrated in *The True Principles*. Overall it was the massive and severe form of the piece, in addition to the stark contrast of its coloured decoration, that made the design so powerful. This bold, even primitive quality of Gothic design was far removed from the refined detail of Pugin's work, although Pugin did design some plain oak furniture for some of his commissions. Nonetheless, it was the primitive and powerful character of designs by the so-called Gothic Reformers of the 1860s and 1870s that sets their work apart from earlier Gothic Revival design.

The popularizer of Reformed Gothic for the discerning middle-class patron was

Bruce Talbert, whose book *Gothic Forms applied to Furniture, Metal Work and Decoration for Domestic Purposes* of 1867–8 was dedicated to G E Street. A Scot like Shaw, Talbert trained as a woodcarver. His love of wood is evident in the Reformed Gothic panelling and furniture illustrated in his book with effects like chamfering, protruding beam ends, and the cutting of repetitive geometric Gothic forms. While owing something to Pugin's ideas, this treatment springs directly from an early commission by Street for sturdy, undeco-rated Gothic furniture for student accom-modation in Cuddesdon College, Oxford.

The remarkable table designed by Street for Cuddesdon had a massive round top of oak with four simple, flat legs, each ending in a silhouette of a trefoil. The raised stretcher in the shape of a Greek cross was designed to penetrate the upright legs, being held in place with wooden pegs. This bold

*An oak baby's cradle designed by Alfred Waterhouse, 1867. Waterhouse produced this design for the infant son of his friend and fellow architect, Richard Norman Shaw. With its bold, simplified shape, it can be linked to the Reformed Gothic.*

use of simple medieval forms by Street was to go far beyond any design by Pugin. Street directly inspired the Gothic Reformers Shaw and Talbert and anticipated the Arts and Crafts designers. For its date of 1854, Street's table was a radical design which was to point the way for the Gothic Reformers. By stripping Gothic forms of their ornament, their designs were ultimately to move away from all but the most general references to medievalism.

In North America, the Reformed Gothic style was to be furthered by an Englishman, Charles Eastlake. He was well-connected in the London art world, being a nephew of the President of the Royal Academy and Director of the National Gallery. During the 1860s he published articles in two leading London magazines on how to furnish a home tastefully. These articles grew into *Hints on Household Taste in Furniture,*

*Upholstery and Other Details* of 1868. The book had gone through six editions by 1881, making it almost as popular as Rickman's book on Gothic architecture. It was widely read in America, where 'Eastlake furniture' meant Gothic Revival furniture.

In fact, although Eastlake was enthusiastic about the Gothic style – he is now remembered as the author of the first history of the Gothic Revival, in 1872 – and included illustrations of his own designs for Reformed Gothic furniture in the book, he did not exclusively recommend the Gothic. In the Preface to the fourth (1878) edition of his book, he wrote: 'I find American tradesmen continually advertising what they are pleased to call 'Eastlake' furniture, with the production of which I had nothing whatever to do, and for the taste of which I should be very sorry to be considered responsible.' In his book Eastlake tried to establish the principles of good design in a variety of objects, including Greek style pottery and Middle Eastern textiles. The eclecticism of Eastlake in using the Gothic simply as one option for the discriminating client was to become increasingly common in the later nineteenth century. Pugin's passionate advocacy of Gothic as the only true style for design did not long outlive him.

In addition to Shaw and Talbert, two other followers of G E Street became Gothic Reformers. They were the architect Philip Webb and the designer and writer William Morris. Webb had joined Street's architectural office in Oxford in 1854, the year the remarkable Cuddesdon College furniture was designed. Two years later he was joined by Morris, a former student of Oxford University, who had rejected a

*The entrance to the Manchester Assize Courts, as published by Charles Eastlake in* A History of the Gothic Revival *(1872). Waterhouse's design of 1859 was chosen from more than a hundred entries to the competition for the Assize Courts, and it was his first important commission in a career distinguished for its civic architecture.*

*Painted cabinet on a stand designed by Philip Webb, the doors decorated by Edward Burne-Jones, made by Morris, Marshall, Faulkner & Co., 1861. Webb trained in the office of G E Street, whose influence can be seen in the design of this Gothic furniture with its massive simplified forms. The extensive use of polychromy to decorate the furniture produced by Morris's firm illustrates the interest of his circle in blurring the distinction between fine and decorative arts.*

career in the Church in favour of pursuing the art theories of John Ruskin. Both Webb and Morris were influenced by *The Stones of Venice*. The two men became close friends in Street's office before leaving in 1857 to begin their design collaboration that was to last for the rest of the century.

Webb's first independent architectural commission was the design of a house for Morris, Red House in Bexleyheath, Kent, in 1859. The house was executed in red brick on an L-shaped plan with windows on the exterior whose irregular placement was dictated by the arrangement of the rooms. This principle of design was antithetical to classical ideals but had long been associated with Gothic Revival architecture. The most immediate precedent for Webb's house was the architecture of Butterfield, but in fact Pugin's first house, St Marie's Grange, in Salisbury, built some 25 years earlier, was perhaps the earliest example of this new type of domestic architecture. Like Pugin's design, Webb's was an attempt to find a formula for a domestic Gothic architecture that did not rely on ecclesiastical forms such as tracery, pinnacles or buttresses. This was in keeping with principles of design advocated first by Pugin and then by Ruskin concerning sound construction and appropriate ornament.

Webb designed the Red House on the occasion of the marriage of his friend in 1859 to the daughter of an Oxford coachman who he had been introduced to by Dante Gabriel Rossetti. Jane Morris shared her husband's passion for things medieval during the early years of their marriage, and she was accomplished in the field of embroidery, helping Morris to study medieval

textiles and embroidery technique. For their first home, Webb designed the forms and Morris the decoration and furnishings to complement Webb's architecture.

Some of these furnishings for the Red House came from the lodgings Morris had shared in London with his great friend from university, Edward Burne-Jones. Rossetti described a 'table and chairs like *incubi* and *succubi*… intensely medieval.' Morris and his friends had also designed an enormous settle with painted decoration which found its way to the Red House. The type was an archaic form of seat furniture of joined panel construction with a tall back that Morris, and the later Arts and Crafts designers, were to revive. Morris's first biographer, J W Mackail, recounts:

*The great painted settle from Red Lion Square was taken and set up in the drawing-room, the top of it being railed in so as to form a small music gallery. Much of the furniture was specially designed by Webb and executed under his eye: the great oak dining table, other tables, chairs, cupboards, massive copper candlesticks, firedogs, and table glass of extreme beauty.*

In 1861 Morris used his own money and contributions from partners to set up a house-decorating business, trading at first under the name Morris, Marshall, Faulkner & Co. He assumed full control in the mid 1860s and the firm became simply Morris & Co. Morris's concept, a co-operative team of craftsmen all sharing in decision-making as well as design and production, was derived from Ruskin's teachings concerning the vibrant handicraft tradition of the Middle Ages. Morris was to use his medievalism as a

*A painted settle-cabinet, 1859–60. This box-like cabinet, designed by Philip Webb, with its integral settle formed part of the furniture at Morris's Red House in Kent, also designed by Webb on the occasion of Morris's marriage. Although some of the finish has been damaged, particularly around the seat, the dark varnish would have simulated the effect of fire blackened oak of medieval times.*

*Opposite: A detail of a mural painting, the Red House, Bexleyheath, Kent, 1860. Using a medieval source for inspiration, Edward Burne-Jones painted a scene of a wedding banquet to honour his friends, William and Jane Morris, who appear here as the king and queen. Medieval art was an important source of inspiration for the Pre-Raphaelite painters, several of whom collaborated with William Morris.*

route to socialism, which he came to espouse as passionately as Pugin had espoused Catholicism. While Pugin had sought to reform design by means of faith, Morris sought to reform society by means of design.

The decorative art produced by the Morris firm, and most particularly his designs for textiles and wallpapers, remain great classics of nineteenth-century design. The work of Morris & Co. in combination with Morris's theories about craftsmanship and design inspired a number of designers in Continental Europe, most notably in Germany. Webb functioned as the consultant architect who designed much of the early furniture in a massive, primitive medieval style. Much of the initial

business of the firm was for ecclesiastical stained glass for the many churches that were being built or restored during the nineteenth century, but gradually the firm's domestic commissions increased. Morris's willingness to investigate every aspect of production and to revive lost techniques (such as dyeing textiles with natural indigo blue) resulted in objects of outstanding beauty and simplicity. By the 1870s, however, the medieval character of the firm's work had faded, in the face of fresh inspiration from the Middle East, antiquity and from other periods of English design.

Increasingly during the 1870s designers such as Shaw, Webb and Morris turned away from the Gothic forms to new areas of design,

*The painted and gilt chimneypiece and a door with gilt metal grille in the Winter Smoking Room at Cardiff Castle, designed by William Burges, 1870. More than any other Gothic Revival architect of his generation, Burges favoured the use of polychromatic decoration and rich, varied materials to create his fantastic interiors.*

*A mahogany side cabinet with mother of pearl and mirrored panels in the Winter Smoking Room, Cardiff Castle.*

*A detail of the ceiling (left) and a view (right) of Lord Bute's Bedroom, Cardiff Castle, designed by William Burges in 1874–5. Burges was deeply interested in Islamic as well as medieval art, as seen here in the interlocking star forms of the ceiling.*

*Opposite: Painted and gilt vaulting in the Winter Smoking Room at Cardiff Castle, 1870. One of Burges's interests was astrology; signs of the zodiac have been set within the six-lobed frame against a ground of gilt stars.*

most notably influences from Japan and other cultures, which gave rise to Aestheticism.

The Arts and Crafts Movement, which looked to the folk, or vernacular, tradition of medieval design, can be viewed as another descendant of the Gothic Revival. This development was paralleled in America, where the Herter Brothers, who began

working in the Gothic style, went on to create an American version of Aestheticism. The American architectural critic H Hudson Holly observed in 1878:

*One of the principles upon which the promoters of the Gothic revival insisted with energy and eloquence was 'truth in architecture'… But the*

*A doorcase in the Banqueting Hall at Cardiff Castle, c1875, designed by William Burges.*

*A view of the Library at Cardiff Castle, c1875. The chimneypiece featured personifications of the ancient languages.*

*Doorcases in the Library. The ogee arches, with their richly cusped leaf decoration, were derived from Burges' study of Flamboyant Gothic on the Continent. They contrast with the simple battlemented forms of the bookcases.*

*Opposite: A detail of the ceiling, the Dining Room at Cardiff Castle, c1874, designed by William Burges. This famous ceiling panel, with its gilded 'jelly mould' form was inspired by examples of Islamic architecture that Burges had seen. The low relief patterned panels surrounding it resemble carved pierced screens in Islamic interiors.*

*The timbered ceiling in the Banqueting Hall recalls that by A W N Pugin in the Great Hall at Scarisbrick. The most impressively medieval in character of all the Cardiff interiors, the Banqueting Hall was a formal room for entertaining. The theme of the mural paintings and chimneypiece was the life of Robert the Consul, Lord of Cardiff Castle in the twelfth century.*

*new reformers say that truth is not the peculiar possession of Gothic architecture.*

From the International Exhibition of 1862 had emerged a great talent of the Gothic Revival who was to lead it to a final blaze of glory. William Burges was able to create a richness and fantasy in his interiors that had been rarely equalled except,

perhaps, by E W Pugin and Bentley at Carlton Towers. Like them, Burges had studied Continental Gothic design, with its richly decorated forms. He had an excellent 'Gothic pedigree', as he had been articled to the architect Edward Blore in the 1840s, and worked in the office of the son of James Wyatt. He began as an Ecclesiologist and helped to design the Medieval Court of the

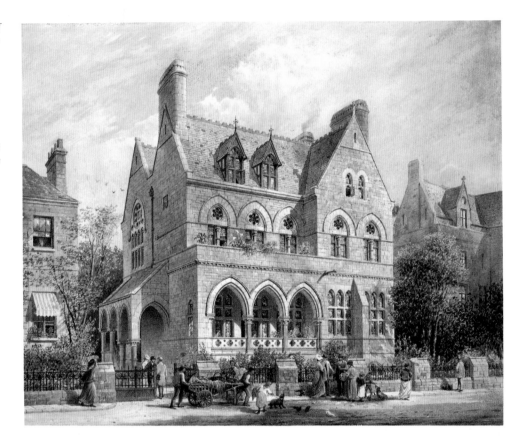

*A drawing by Axel Haig of the entrance façade, House for James McConnochie, Park Place, Cardiff, designed by William Burges, 1871–80. The large areas of masonry and deeply-cut openings into the wall surface link William Burges's domestic architecture to the category of 'muscular Gothic', as defined by Robert Kerr in 1864.*

1862 Exhibition in London. During the 1840s and 50s he acquired a considerable knowledge of medieval metalwork and decorative art, and he falls within the category of 'antiquarian' architects of the Gothic Revival. He executed few buildings, as his rich, fantastic Gothic style required equally rich patrons, but his finished works are outstanding monuments to nineteenth-century Gothic. The most important of these are Cardiff Castle and his own residence, Tower House, in London.

The great patron of William Burges was the romantically minded third Marquess of Bute, who had converted to Catholicism in 1868, the year he came of age and acquired an enormous fortune. He shared the passion of Burges and others before him for the Gothic as an alternative vision to the industrial reality of Victorian Britain. In 1868 Burges was employed to rebuild the medieval castle at Cardiff as the fantasy residence of one of the richest young men in Britain. Work continued for nearly 20 years. The massive, stout walls and the use of bold, geometric shapes place it firmly within Kerr's category of 'muscular' Gothic.

A painted Cabinet on a
Stand, 1875. William
Burges was one of the
antiquarian designers
fascinated by the discovery
by Viollet-le-Duc of a
medieval cabinet with its
painted decoration intact.
The use of allegorical figures
outlined in black against a
patterned ground, as seen
here, was to become a regular
feature of his painted
furniture.

*A detail of the chimneypiece in the Drawing Room, Tower House, London, by William Burges, 1875–87. Thomas Nicholls executed much of the sculptural decoration for Burges at Tower House.*

*Opposite: The exterior of Tower House, Melbury Road, London. When Cardiff Castle was well under way for the Marquess of Bute, Burges began to build his own house in London, a masterpiece of his 'muscular Gothic' in miniature.*

*A view of the Library, Tower House, London. The sculptor Nicholls made the remarkable, castle-like chimneypiece, with its fire surround of alabaster.*

In striking contrast to the severe, fortress-like exterior, the interiors of Cardiff Castle were riotous in their colourful medievalism. Burges used a rich mixture of media, including stone and plaster details, figurative painting and gilding, woodwork, tiles, metalwork, and stencilled designs. His materials were of the highest quality, and his designs were full of invention and imagination. Burges was a close friend of the Pre-Raphaelite painter Dante Gabriel Rossetti, and the narrative quality of Rossetti's paintings can be seen in Burges's designs.

For the washstand of his guest bedroom in Tower House, named 'Vita Nuova' after a poem by Dante that had also inspired Rossetti, Burges designed a beautiful bowl of alabaster that tipped up to empty the washing water into a bucket below, while inlaid into the stone were silver fishes that appeared to swim lazily when the wash basin was full of water. The tap itself was a literal rendering of a bronze aquamanile which was used in the Middle Ages by priests for the ceremonial washing of hands. A number of fine examples have survived from the Middle Ages, and Burges would have known about this type. One could argue that this demonstrates 'appropriateness' of ornament, although Pugin would doubtless have considered this design to lack propriety.

The architect and biographer of Philip Webb, William Lethaby, likened Burges to a court jester. The characterization is also apt when considering the spirit of Burges's work. Unlike Pugin, he was not seriously concerned with questions of faith or ideology. Unlike Morris, he was not concerned with the reform of design or society. He was a dedicated antiquarian, something of a reactionary in his own age, and he displayed a high-spirited sense of fun in his work. It was glorious while it lasted, but he founded no school of design and trained no further generation of Gothic designers. Cardiff Castle was the last great masterpiece of the Gothic Revival.

*Two details of exterior stonework at Knightshayes Court, Devon, by William Burges, 1867–74. These stylized leaves and heads in the Early English Gothic of the thirteenth century recall examples at Salisbury Cathedral. Burges designed the house, but J D Crace (the son of Pugin's partner) was called in to design the interiors, owing to the high cost of executing Burges's design.*

*Opposite: A detail of the sculptural decoration in the Drawing Room of the Tower House, London. The talent of Thomas Nicholls is revealed in the modelling of these figures in a neo-Gothic style. The theme is taken from the great medieval epic,* The Romance of the Rose.

Although Burges trained in Britain and was well-known to British designers, his rich, colourful style of Gothic had stronger links with Continental Europe than with British Gothic design. A trip to France in 1867 was especially influential. Burges visited the Château Pierrefonds in Picardy, northern France, a medieval ruin being rebuilt as a residence for the Emperor Napoleon III in an overt piece of architectural propaganda as an attempt to establish the right to rule of the nephew of the first Napoleon. The architect was Eugène Viollet-le-Duc, who was in charge of the restoration of Notre Dame Cathedral and the Sainte Chapelle in Paris, two of the most famous of thirteenth-century French Gothic monuments. Viollet-le-Duc was

deeply involved with the reintroduction of polychromatic decoration to medieval interiors and with the study and restoration of medieval stained glass. Pierrefonds was richly decorated with sculpted and painted ornament taken from a wide variety of periods of medieval art, including Norman architecture from Sicily. This eclectic approach to the Gothic was used by Burges.

Burges freely acknowledged his debt, commenting that 'we all cribbed from Viollet-le-Duc.' In particular, his furniture designs were inspired by a painted medieval armoire, or textile cupboard, published by Viollet-le-Duc in a French archaeological journal in the 1840s. Existing examples of medieval furniture with their decoration intact were very rare, and Viollet-le-Duc's

*An exterior view towards the Entrance Tower, Château of Pierrefonds, Picardy, France, remodelled by Eugène Viollet-le-Duc, 1858–65. Viollet restored the late medieval castle for Emperor Napoleon III, who was anxious to 'legitimize' his reign by means of architectural symbols. The interiors were in Viollet's rich mix of medieval styles of design.*

*Opposite: A view of the Château of Pierrefonds, Picardy, France, by Jean-Baptiste Camille Corot, c1840. Corot painted Pierrefonds before Viollet-le-Duc's restoration when it was still a ruin and formed a picturesque subject for this landscape.*

article caused a stir in antiquarian circles. For his furniture designs, Burges adopted the box-like forms and stylized painted decoration illustrated by Viollet-le-Duc. The Vita Nuova washstand, for example, was made in the form of an upright box on four simple, straight legs, with a few deeply cut Gothic motifs and long metal strap hinges. The richness of the design was in the materials and painted decoration used, but the form of the piece itself was primitive and owed its inspiration to Viollet-le-Duc's article.

However, Viollet's own Gothic style furniture for Pierrefonds and for other commissions was to look quite different, with its long, sinuous lines and riotous naturalistic ornament of scrolling leaves carved into the oak of the frame. The books on art that Viollet-le-Duc began to publish in the 1860s stressed that the designer must look to the underlying principles of medieval design rather than simply reproducing medieval forms. He was deeply concerned that nineteenth-century designers should develop a style that was expressive of their own era. Ultimately, Viollet-le-Duc's pupils were to become the pioneers of Art Nouveau, that most distinctive of early twentieth-century styles, whereas his greatest admirer

in Spain, Antonio Gaudì, was to unite the Gothic with the surreal in his extraordinary mass of concrete pinnacles and gables – the unfinished Cathedral of the Holy Family, or Sagrada Familia, in Barcelona.

Viollet-le-Duc had considerable influence in promoting appreciation for the Gothic in Europe. In 1867, the year Burges had visited Pierrefonds, a young Bavarian prince, Ludwig II (later to be known as 'Mad Ludwig') visited the stronghold of Napoleon III and was so delighted with it he used it as the inspiration for his own fairy-tale castle, Neuschwanstein, set in the dramatic foothills of the Bavarian Alps. The dates of Neuschwanstein exactly overlap those of Cardiff Castle – about 1867 to 1885. However, in contrast to Burges's talented and original handling of the Gothic style, Ludwig II employed a team of theatrical designers who made his castle look like the set of a Wagnerian opera. Wagner, in fact, did stay nearby in the more tasteful Gothic retreat of Hohenschwangau, an

1820s rebuilding of a medieval hunting lodge for the princes of Bavaria. The theatrical Neuschwanstein did inspire one descendant: the original Disneyland Castle in Anaheim, California, built in the 1950s, which has since become a symbol of popular culture in the twentieth century.

Where, then, did the Gothic style stand at the close of the nineteenth century? William Morris was dead, but had long ago left his medieval designs behind. His followers were now the social reformers of the Arts and Crafts Movement. William Burges did not live to see Cardiff Castle completed, and 'Mad Ludwig' was found drowned in a lake, at which point work on Neuschwanstein was suspended. Viollet-le-Duc was also dead, his pupils inventing the Art Nouveau. Even J F Bentley, who had taken over the interiors of Carlton Towers from E W Pugin, was now working in the Byzantine style. While continuing in church and collegiate architecture, the Gothic style was in decline for domestic buildings by 1900.

By 1900 the Gothic style was rarely used in domestic architecture. In Britain it had been overtaken during the final quarter of the nineteenth century by Philip Webb's 'Old English' and Richard Norman Shaw's 'Queen Anne' style, which produced the large, comfortable houses evoking the vernacular styles of the past then in fashion among British patrons of new houses. Ecclesiastical and collegiate architecture continued to rely upon the Gothic style, however. The grandson of George Gilbert Scott, Giles Gilbert Scott, continued to use the Gothic for a surprising number of commissions in the twentieth century, beginning with his winning the design for the new Liverpool Cathedral in 1904 at the age of 24. With the exception of the bold, massive Battersea Power Station in London, built early in the 1930s, he was known for his designs for churches or colleges, where the Gothic was already an established style.

In the USA the architect Ralph Cram helped to keep the Gothic tradition alive. He published *The Gothic Quest* in 1907, followed by *The Substance of Gothic* in 1917. His best known work is undoubtedly the monumental Cathedral of St John the Divine in New York, begun in 1911 in a crisp French Rayonnant Gothic style. Of similar date and style is the Princeton University Chapel in New Jersey, dedicated in 1928. (Cram also designed the Graduate College of Princeton.) In the precise cutting and

*Lacock Abbey, Wiltshire,
painted by John Piper, 1940.
In this moody oil painting,
Piper has highlighted the
ogee arched gateway and
entrance façade designed
by Sanderson Miller. The
long medieval history of
the building is evoked here,
while Piper's interest in the
Romantic Movement of
the nineteenth century is
evident.*

tooling of the masonry in his work, and the exact repetition of elements such as window tracery, Cram's work exemplifies the competent but rather monotonous quality of much twentieth-century Gothic.

One outstandingly imaginative twentieth-century interpretation of medievalism can be found in Devon, England: Edwin Lutyens's Castle Drogo, set high upon a spectacular site overlooking the River Teign. The house was built over a 20-year period between 1910 and 1930, and in fact was never entirely finished. The fortress-like building was designed for a family with a strong interest in the medieval period, and Lutyens's use of roughly-cut blocks of stone, variegated in colour, created a most imposing structure that appears to have withstood centuries of weather. With a battlemented roofline, large, high windows with grid-like tracery and details such as a little chapel with a belfry built into the massive castle walls, Castle Drogo is a rare example of a bold, fresh, and vigorous re-interpretation of the Gothic architectural tradition in the twentieth century.

Since 1945, limited use has been made of the Gothic tradition in architecture. Scattered examples of ecclesiastical and collegiate Gothic can be found, particularly in North America, while in Anaheim, California, Walt Disney had a Gothic castle built in 1950 as the centre of the new Disneyland. In Britain an outstanding post-war example of the Gothic tradition is Castle Gyrn in Wales, built by the architect John Taylor for himself and finished in 1977. Castle Gyrn has a compact design of rectangular and square-shaped blocks executed in bold and irregularly-sized stones, deeply cut

windows of varied geometrical shapes, and battlementing.

In many respects, the twentieth century represents a period of Gothic Survival, rather than Revival, as was the case in the seventeenth century. Instances where the Gothic style has been used can also often be traced to historical circumstance or established stylistic traditions. For example, Sir Michael Blake engaged the painter and designer Felix Kelly to remodel his house in the Gothic style, reflecting the design of his demolished family seat, the eighteenth-century house at Tillmouth Park, Northumberland. Kelly remodelled the Dower House on the estate in a 1970s version of eighteenth-century Gothic that owes much to the designs of Batty Langley and Horace Walpole. The Dower House can be seen as an example of the twentieth-century Gothic Survival. Neither it nor Castle Gyrn, however, are part of a larger design movement towards the Gothic. The situation is the same as regards the design of furnishings, with a few exceptions, such as Rupert Williamson's design for an updated version of a Gothic chair for the Chapel of Milton Manor, Oxfordshire, a house with eighteenth-century Gothic interiors.

As the Gothic has waned as an active style of design in this century, it has increased as a focus of interest for scholars and conservationists, echoing the rise in scholarship of the Gothic during the seventeenth century. During the inter-war period, two important books were published that revived interest in and awareness of the style. In 1928 the art historian Kenneth Clark published *The Gothic Revival: an Essay in the History of Taste*, the first book

*Opposite: Castle Drogo, Devon, from the south, by Cyril Farey, c1923. Castle Drogo is a rare modern masterpiece of castellated architecture. Edwin Lutyens designed the castle early in the twentieth century using bold, cliff-like granite walls, grid-like windows, and on the north side, massive battlements. Castle Drogo represents a highly successful meeting of the medieval building tradition with the modern age.*

*Following pages: A reconstruction of the West Front Screen at Exeter Cathedral, Devon by Stephen Conlin based upon the research of Eddie Sinclair, 1993. The enormous west screen represents the Jesse Tree or genealogy of Christ. When first installed in 1450, it was richly painted. A W N Pugin and his contemporaries knew that medieval architecture was highly polychromatic, but it was not until the twentieth century that advanced methods of technological analysis enabled scholars and conservators to make very accurate models of the medieval use of colour.*

CASTLE DROGO

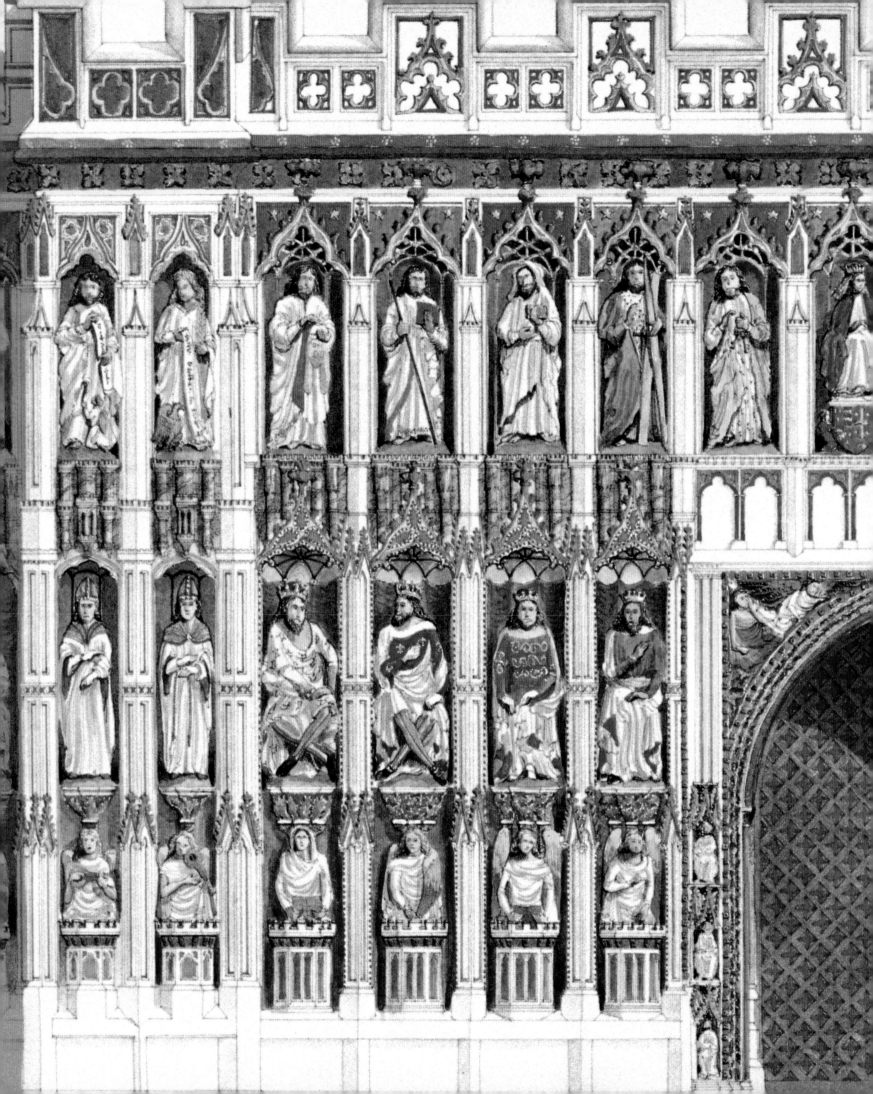

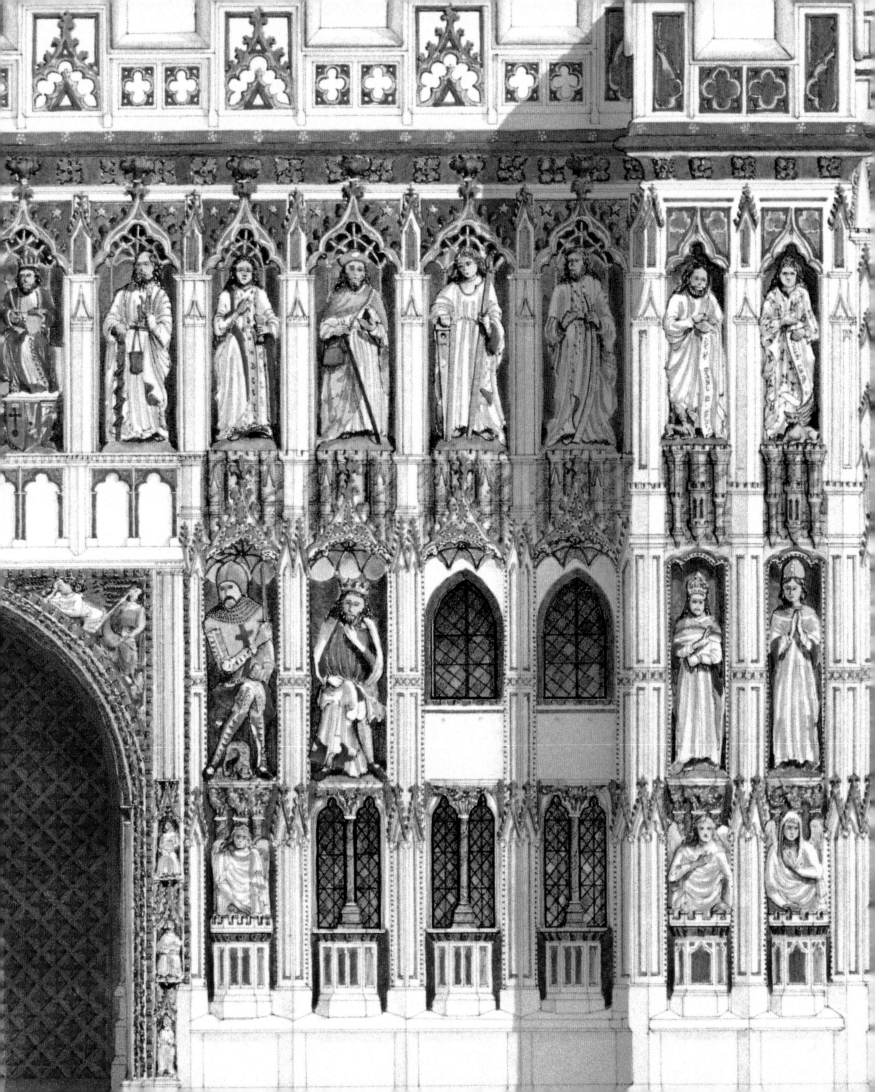

*A modern colourway of a wallpaper designed by A W N Pugin, c1845–8. Known as the 'Gothic Sun' pattern, this was reproduced by Perry's of Islington for the Palace of Westminster. The extensive programme of restoration carried out at the Palace during the 1970s saw the reproduction of A W N Pugin's designs for carpets, wallpapers and textiles, some of which are available commercially. The cobalt blue ground of this paper is one of the deep, clear colours that Pugin helped to popularize.*

*A modern colourway of a wallpaper produced by Cole and Son of London, mid-nineteenth century. The stylized pomegranate and leaf design illustrates how the design of Pugin inspired less radical, more commercial versions of the Gothic in the nineteenth century.*

*A modern colourway of a wallpaper designed by A W N Pugin, 1847, for the New Palace of Westminster. Known as the 'Crace Diaper', this simple trellis pattern with Gothic rosettes was used widely by J G Crace in his house-decorating business in the nineteenth century.*

*A modern colourway of a wallpaper produced by Cole and Son, mid-nineteenth century, using a stylized trellis design.*

*The Gothic Villa, Regents Park, London, 1991. The design of this villa by Quinlan Terry echoes the eighteenth-century practice of adding Gothic-style details to an exterior that is of classical shape and proportions. The most prominent Gothic details seen here are the battlements, pinnacles and dripstone mouldings, with a quatrefoil window inscribed within the gable of the facade. Terry's work has consistently looked to eighteenth-century sources for inspiration.*

on the subject since that of Charles Eastlake in 1872. Shortly afterwards in 1936 the architectural and design historian Nikolaus Pevsner published *Pioneers of the Modern Movement*. Both were seminal books, Clark's exploring the relationship of the Gothic to literature and antiquarianism, Pevsner's highlighting the leading role that Gothic Revival architects had played in developing the avant-garde styles of the late nineteenth and early twentieth centuries.

Gothic Revival buildings have suffered much from a lack of understanding and appreciation during the recent past. The founding of the Victorian Society in Britain in 1958 was of great importance in the preservation of existing Gothic Revival buildings, many of which had stood empty after the Second World War, and in assuaging the destruction of these buildings in the 1960s. The recent and thorough programme of restoration at the Palace of Westminster has resulted in the revival of its splendid decorative designs by Pugin and has encouraged interest for the Gothic style wallpapers, carpets and furniture amongst a small group of collectors and antiquarians.

Thanks in part to a growing popular enthusiasm for architectural conservation, historically based styles and ornament are once more in fashion. The work of Gothic Revival architects is attracting a growing legion of admirers who appreciate the richness of Gothic forms and the evocative, literary qualities of the style. Perhaps a future literary movement whose practitioners focus on the supernatural, the spiritual, and the remote, may in time spark another revival of Gothic design.

ARCADING

A succession of arches carried on piers or columns. Arcading can be used structurally, as in the nave of a cathedral, or decoratively, as in the rich stone ornament of Gothic architecture.

BATTLEMENT

Originally a device for fortifying medieval architecture. A battlement is a PARAPET with indentations through which those manning the building could shoot. (Also called crenellation.)

BAY

A unit of interior architectural space, such as a bay in the nave of a Gothic cathedral; also a projecting window.

BOARD AND BATTEN

A form of vertical wooden siding on North American architecture. This technique was developed from the horizontal clapboarding found on the vernacular architecture of the Middle Ages in England.

BUTTRESS

An exterior projecting unit of masonry or brickwork built against a wall to give it strength. (See also FLYING BUTTRESS.)

CAPITAL

The top, or upper, portion of a column or COLONNETTE which can be decorated in a variety of ways. Gothic capitals usually featured leaf ornament.

CARPENTER'S GOTHIC

Essentially a folk interpretation of Gothic designs in wood, seen in churches, houses and furnishings, and found principally in North America during the mid-nineteenth century.

CASTELLATION

Literally, to make like a castle, normally by means of features such as BATTLEMENTS and TURRETS. (Hence CASTELLATED.)

CHAMFERING

The cutting of a plane on the diagonal,

across a right angle, to create a polygonal silhouette. Chamfering was much used in Gothic architecture and in Reformed Gothic designs of the nineteenth century.

CHOIR

The space within a church or cathedral that is situated immediately east of the nave and is often separated by a screen. The clergy and singers assembled in the choir, where the service was held.

CLERESTORY

The upper storey of a NAVE elevation, containing windows.

CLOISTER

A quadrangular, covered walkway normally attached to a cathedral or abbey to facilitate passage from the church to other buildings of the foundation. Cloisters seem to have been used as places of contemplation and recreation in the Middle Ages.

COLONNETTE

A slender column that was used decoratively in Gothic architecture to express the force exerted by the RIBS of the VAULTING.

CROCKET

A small decorative ornament consisting of leaf shapes modelled in a tightly curled profile, used in Gothic architecture. Crockets were often used to decorate PINNACLES or GABLES.

CUSP

Projecting points, sometimes abstract, sometimes stylized leaves, that interrupt the curve of a Gothic arch, making its silhouette more complex.

DAIS

A raised platform used for the seating of a person of exalted rank.

DIAPER

A trellis-like pattern which can consist of squares or lozenges, often filled with stylized flower heads.

DRIPSTONE MOULDING

A Late Gothic type of stone moulding used above windows and doorways to direct water away from the openings in the wall.

ENCAUSTIC

A medieval method of tile-making revived in the nineteenth century by Herbert Minton, whereby coloured clay was inlaid into a terracotta ground before it was dry.

FLYING BUTTRESS

A BUTTRESS that is anchored to the main body of a building by means of transverse arches which appear to 'fly' through space, without visible supports.

FOLIATED

Decorated with leaf ornament (from the Latin).

GABLE

The triangularly shaped upper end of the wall of a building under the lines of the pointed roof.

GOTHIC ARCHITECTURE

A style of building that arose in Northern France during the second half of the twelfth century and remained in use until the beginning of the sixteenth century (characterized by the pointed arch and VAULTING). Gothic masons broke the round arch of the preceding Romanesque period into two (or later, four) intersecting arcs of a circle, giving rise to a flexible system of construction that created vaulted interiors of unprecedented height and reduced wall mass to a minimum by the use of arcades and windows. The first Gothic structure is considered to be the choir of the abbey church at St Denis, north of Paris, begun in 1144.

GOTHIC NOVEL

A genre of literature that developed during the second half of the eighteenth century, emphasizing elements of supernatural power and often using remote settings in the medieval period. Horace Walpole is credited with having

written the first Gothic novel, *The Castle of Otranto*, which was published in 1764.

GOTHIC REVIVAL

A phenomenon in architecture, design and literature of the eighteenth and nineteenth centuries involving the re-use of a wide range of medieval styles of architecture and references to the Middle Ages. The Gothic Revival developed out of antiquarian studies and scholarly literature of the later seventeenth century.

GOTHIC SURVIVAL

A phenomenon of the seventeenth century in which Gothic forms of architecture were actively used, particularly for the restoration of churches and for the Oxbridge colleges.

GOTHICK ARCHITECTURE

Some modern writers use the archaic spelling of Gothic to signify the early revival – essentially the eighteenth century.

HALL

In medieval MANOR houses the principal, if not the only, living space of a household. Later on the Great Hall became associated with banquets and public assemblies.

KEEP

The central, usually massive, block within a castle compound to which a final retreat could be made in times of siege. The Normans were famed for the strength of their keeps. (Also called a donjon.)

LANCET

A slender, vertical form (usually with a pointed arch) found in window TRACERY and used as a decorative feature in Gothic architecture.

LATIN CROSS

A cross in which the lowest projecting arm is the longest, as opposed to the Greek cross, where each arm is of equal length.

MANOR
A domestic residence in the Middle Ages, usually of a land-owner or farmer. Manor houses could be modest in scale, and for security's sake the principal rooms were usually above ground, on the first floor.

NAVE
The main interior space of a church or cathedral, running without interruption from the west entrance to the altar; usually flanked by aisles.

OGEE ARCH
A bowed, or four-centred arch whose summit is composed of two elongated S-shaped curves. The ogee arch is commonly found in Late Gothic architecture and in eighteenth-century Gothic Revival design.

OLD ENGLISH
See TUDOR.

ORIEL
Either a polygonal, projecting bay window; or a small chamber containing an oriel window. Originally the oriel was a place of prayer, but it became a secular feature in the later medieval period.

PARAPET
A low wall usually along the roofline of a building, often BATTLEMENTED in the Middle Ages.

PENDANT
A decorative feature of English Perpendicular Gothic vaulting, much copied in ceilings during the Gothic Revival.

PICTURESQUE
An aesthetic concept which arose during the eighteenth century whereby the landscape garden began to be arranged with studied informality and variety, in the manner of a 'picture'. Picturesque design was translated from the garden to architecture, and the quest for visual variety occasionally led to THE SUBLIME.

PIER
A large vertical support of stone often composed of a cluster of COLONNETTES. (Sometimes called a 'pillar' in older texts.)

PINNACLE
A vertical ornament, probably derived from the Romanesque TURRET, that is polygonal in shape, often with a tapering top, and placed on top of structural elements in the Gothic exterior. By its weight, the pinnacle helped to stabilize a structure. Gothic pinnacles were often decorated with CROCKETS.

POLYCHROMY
Literally 'many colours', polychromy could be achieved by means of painting or the use of variously coloured building materials. Once scholars discovered that ancient buildings and furniture had been richly coloured, the re-creation of polychromatic decoration became a central aspect of the Gothic Revival in the nineteenth century.

PORTAL
The entrance to a church or cathedral. Principal portals were always on the west facade and could be elaborately decorated with programmes of sculpture.

QUATREFOIL
A Gothic ornament in the shape of a four-lobed flower. (See also TREFOIL.)

RAMPART
A wall surrounding a castle, fort or city, used for defence.

REFORMED GOTHIC
A Gothic style of the 1860s and 70s which emphasized the use of bold silhouettes and massive construction, with repetitive geometric ornament. Reformed Gothic was an attempt to leave behind the sophisticated fifteenth-century Gothic style in favour of a more vigorous approach to design.

RIB
A projecting moulding on a vault or ceiling, used structurally or decoratively. (See also VAULTING.)

ROMANTIC MOVEMENT
A phenomenon in European culture with roots in the eighteenth century which came to fruition during the first third of the nineteenth century. The Romantic Movement was a shift away from the rational principles of thought of the Renaissance, when it was felt that Nature could be explained by fixed and observable principles, to the idea that Nature had a mysterious and unfathomable force that could not be controlled.

RUINATION
The process of designing a structure to look as though it had decayed over time. Ruined monuments became fashionable in the eighteenth century with the advent of PICTURESQUE landscape design.

SCOTTISH BARONIAL ARCHITECTURE
A genre of the Gothic Revival featuring the round turrets and conical caps typical of Scottish fortified domestic architecture of the late medieval period.

STRAP HINGES
Elongated metal hinges which resemble leather straps, sometimes exaggerated in scale. They were a feature of medieval furniture construction revived by A W N Pugin in the 1840s and used thereafter in the Gothic Revival.

STUMP COLUMNS
Short sections of columns in small scale used as a decorative motif on REFORMED GOTHIC furniture.

THE SUBLIME
An aesthetic category first defined by Edmund Burke in 1757, pertaining to powerful visual effects (such as great height) and evoking a feeling of awe in the viewer.

TRACERY
The often highly decorative network of stone mouldings used to hold the glass within stained glass windows. Tracery was also applied 'blind' to Gothic architecture as a purely decorative feature. QUATREFOILS, TREFOILS and LANCETS were commonly used motifs.

TREFOIL
A three-lobed form commonly found in Gothic ornament. (See also QUATREFOIL.)

TUDOR
The latest period of Gothic design in England (the fifteenth and early sixteenth centuries) which also encompassed the brief Renaissance and lengthier Mannerist period in design. In nineteenth-century domestic architecture 'Tudor' style signified the revival of black and white timbered houses.

TURRET
Essentially a small tower that is usually not free-standing but serves a decorative function in a design.

VAULTING
A system of roofing over an interior space, usually executed in stone, in which the weight of the roof is suspended upon a system of RIBS, which act like a skeleton. Vaulting became increasingly sophisticated from the fourteenth century, when the framework of ribs evolved into an elaborate system combining the decorative with the structural.

VERANDAH
A North American feature in domestic buildings consisting of a long porch with a roof, not enclosed, that often runs the length of one side of a building.

VILLA
In the eighteenth and nineteenth centuries, a detached house, usually on the outskirts of a town, ranking between a cottage and a mansion, with a garden that (as A J Downing remarked) was built to express the taste of its owner.

**For general reading and reference**

Clark, Kenneth. *The Gothic Revival: An Essay in the History of Taste*. 3rd ed. London: John Murray, 1962.

Eastlake, Charles. *A History of the Gothic Revival*. J M Crook, ed. Leicester: The University Press, 1971.

Fleming, John, Honour, Hugh, and Pevsner, Nikolaus. *The Penguin Dictionary of Architecture*. 4th ed. Harmondsworth: Penguin Books, 1991.

Germann, Georg. *Gothic Revival in Europe and Britain: Sources, Influences and Ideas*. London: Lund Humphries, 1972.

Hitchcock, Henry Russell. *The Pelican History of Art. Architecture: Nineteenth and Twentieth Centuries*. Harmondsworth: Penguin Books, 1977.

Jervis, Simon. *The Penguin Dictionary of Design and Designers*. Harmondsworth: Penguin Books, 1984.

Parker, John Henry. *A Concise History of Architectural Terms*. London, Studio Editions, 1992.

**Some Gothic novels (available in modern editions)**

Austen, Jane. *Northanger Abbey* (1818).
Beckford, William. *Vathek* (1786).
Polidori, John. *The Vampyre* (1819).
Radcliffe, Ann. *The Mysteries of Udolpho* (1794).
  *The Romance of the Forest* (1791).
Scott, Walter. *Ivanhoe, A Romance* (1819).
  *Tales of the Crusaders*. 4 volumes (1825).
Shelley, Mary. *Frankenstein; or, the Modern Prometheus* (1816).
Shelley, Percy. *Zastrozzi* (1810).
  *St Irvyne; or, the Rosicrucian* (1811).
Stoker, Bram. *Dracula* (1897).
Walpole, Horace. *The Castle of Otranto, A Gothic Story* (1764).

**Chapter 1**
**Gothic Forms and Gothic Sensibilities**

Boccador, Jacqueline. *Le Mobilier Français du Moyen Age à la Renaissance*. St Just: Éditions d'Art Monelle Hayot, 1988.

Eames, Elizabeth S. *Medieval Tiles: A Handbook*. London: British Museum Publications, 1968.

Eames, Penelope. *Medieval Furniture*. London: Furniture History Society, 1977.

James, John. *Chartres: The Masons who built a Legend*. London: Routledge and Kegan Paul, 1985.

Jantzen, Hans. *High Gothic: the Classic Cathedrals of Chartres, Reims, Amiens*. James Palmes, trans. London: Constable & Co., 1962.

Panofsky, Erwin, ed. *Abbot Suger on the Abbey Church of St-Denis and its Art Treasures*. 2nd ed. Princeton: Princeton University Press, 1979.

Stoddard, Whitney S. *Art and Architecture in Medieval France*. New York: Icon Editions, 1972.

Wilson, Christopher. *The Gothic Cathedral: The Architecture of the Great Church, 1130–1530*. Rev. ed. London: Thames and Hudson, 1992.

Wood, Margaret. *The English Medieval House*. Preface by Mortimer Wheeler. London: Bracken Books, 1983.

**Chapter 2**
**Picturesque Landscapes and Gothic Villas**

The Georgian Group, London. *A Gothick Symposium*. London: The Georgian Group, 1983.

Macauley, James. *The Gothic Revival, 1745–1845*. Glasgow: Blackie and Sons, 1975.

McCarthy, Michael. *The Origins of the Gothic Revival*. New Haven and London: Yale University Press, 1987.

Royal Pavilion, Art Gallery and Museums, Brighton. *Gothick, 1720–1840*. Exhib. cat. Brighton: Royal Pavilion, Art Gallery and Museums, 1975.

Walpole, Horace. *A Description of Strawberry Hill*. London: T Kirgate, 1784.

Watkin, David. *The English Vision: The Picturesque in Architecture, Landscape and Garden Design*. London: John Murray, 1982.

Wilson, Michael. *William Kent: Architect, Designer, Painter and Gardener,*

*1685–1748*. London: Routledge and Kegan Paul, 1984.

**Chapter 3**
**Romantic Gothic:**
**Abbeys and Castles**

Austin, Sarah, trans. *A Regency Visitor: the English Tour of Prince Pückler-Muskau Described in His Letters, 1826–1828*. E M Butler, ed. London: Collins, 1957.

Britton, John. *Graphical and Literary Illustrations of Fonthill Abbey*. London: John Britton, 1823.

Lindstrum, Derek. *Sir Jeffry Wyatville, Architect to the King*. Oxford: Oxford University Press, 1972.

Robinson, John Martin. *The Wyatts, An Architectural Dynasty*. Oxford: Oxford University Press, 1979.

Wainwright, Clive. *The Romantic Interior: the British Collector at Home, 1750–1850*. New Haven and London: Yale University Press, 1989.

**Chapter 4**
**Pattern Books and Villas:**
**Gothic for the Middle Classes**

Ackerman, James S. *The Villa: Form and Ideology of Country Houses*. London: Thames and Hudson, 1990.

Andrews, Wayne. *American Gothic: Its Origins, Its Trials, Its Triumphs*. New York: Vintage Books, 1975.

Downing, Andrew Jackson. *Victorian Cottage Residences*. Reprint ed. New York: Dover Publications, 1981.

Guinness, Desmond and Ryan, William. *Irish Houses and Castles*. London: Irish Georgian Society and Thames and Hudson, 1971.

Howe, Katherine S. and Warren, David B. *The Gothic Revival Style in America, 1830–1870*. Jane B Davies, intro. Exhib. cat. Houston: The Museum of Fine Arts, 1976.

Irish Architectural Archive. *The Architecture of Richard Morrison and William Vitruvius Morrison*. Dublin: The Irish Architectural Archive, 1989.

Myles, Janet. *L N Cottingham, 1787–1847: Architect of the Gothic Revival*. London:

Lund Humphries, 1996.

Peck, Amelia, ed. *Alexander Jackson Davis: American Architect, 1803–1892*. Jane B. Davies, intro. New York: The Metropolitan Museum of Art, 1992.

Rickman, Thomas. *An Attempt to Discriminate the Styles of Architecture in England from the Conquest to the Reformation*. 7th ed. Oxford and London: Parker and Co., 1881.

**Chapter 5**
**Gothic Archaeology and Gothic Propriety**

Aldrich, Megan, ed. *The Craces: Royal Decorators, 1769–1899*. London: John Murray, 1990.

Atterbury, Paul, ed. *A W N Pugin, Master of Gothic*. New Haven and London: Yale University Press, 1995.

Atterbury, Paul and Wainwright, Clive, eds. *Pugin: A Gothic Passion*. New Haven and London: Yale University Press, 1994.

Ferrey, Benjamin. *Recollections of Pugin*. Clive Wainwright, intro. London: The Scolar Press, 1978.

Port, M H, ed. *The Houses of Parliament*. New Haven and London, Yale University Press, 1976.

Pugin, A W N. *An Apology for the Revival of Christian Architecture*. London: John Weale, 1843.

Pugin, A W N. *The True Principles of Pointed, or Christian Architecture*. London: John Weale, 1841.

Steegman, John. *Victorian Taste: A Study of the Arts and Architecture from 1830 to 1870*. New ed. London: The National Trust, 1987.

The Lord Sudeley, ed. *The Sudeleys, Lords of Toddington*. London: Manorial Society of Great Britain, 1987.

Wedgwood, Alexandra. *Catalogue of the Drawings Collection of the Royal Institute of British Architects. The Pugin Family*. Farnborough: Gregg International, 1977.

Wedgwood, Alexandra. *Catalogues of the Architectural Drawings in the Victoria and Albert Museum: A W N Pugin and the Pugin Family*. London: Victoria and Albert Museum, 1985.

**Chapter 6**
**Gothic Reform and Gothic Fantasy**
Academy Editions. *Eugène Emmanuel Viollet-le-duc, 1814–1879.* Architectural Design Profile series. London: Academy Editions, 1980.
Cooper, Jeremy. *Victorian and Edwardian Furniture and Interiors from the Gothic Revival to Art Nouveau.* London: Thames and Hudson, 1987.
Crook, J M. *William Burges and the High Victorian Dream.* London: John Murray, 1981.
Eastlake, Charles. *Hints on Household Taste.* Reprint ed. John Gloag, intro. New York: Dover Publications, 1969.
Girouard, Mark. *The Victorian Country House.* Rev. ed. New Haven and London: Yale University Press, 1979.
Hearn, M F (ed.). *The Architectural Theory of Viollet-le-Duc: Readings and Commentary.* Cambridge, Mass.: MIT Press, 1990.
Lethaby, W R. *Philip Webb and his Work.* New ed. London: Raven Oak Press, 1979.
Lewis, Michael J. *The Politics of the German Gothic Revival: August Reichensperger.* Cambridge, Mass.: MIT Press, 1993.
Parry, Linda, ed. *William Morris.* London: Victoria and Albert Museum/Philip Wilson, 1996.
Poulson, Christine. *William Morris.* London: Chartwell Books, 1989.
Ruskin, John. *The Stones of Venice.* J G Links, ed. New York: Hill and Wang, 1960.
Street, G E. *Brick and Marble in the Middle Ages: Notes of a Tour in the North of Italy.* London: John Murray, 1855.
Summerson, John. *Heavenly Mansions and Other Essays on Architecture.* London: W W Norton, 1963.
Thompson, Paul. *William Butterfield.* London: Routledge & Kegan Paul, 1971.
Watkinson, Ray. *William Morris as Designer.* New York: Van Nostrand Reinhold, 1967.

**Sources of information in the UK and Ireland**

Furniture History Society
c/o Dept of Furniture
Victoria and Albert Museum
Cromwell Road
London SW7 2RL

Georgian Group
37 Spital Square
London E1 6DY

Irish Architectural Archive
73 Merrion Square
Dublin 2
Eire

Irish Georgian Society
42 Merrion Square
Dublin 2
Eire

William Morris Society (chapters in Canada, USA and Australia)
26 Upper Mall
London W6 9TA

National Monuments Record (separate bodies for England, Wales and Scotland)
RCHME National Monuments Record
55 Blandford Street
London W1H 3AF

National Trust (UK)
36 Queen Anne's Gate
London SW1H 9AJ

Society for the Protection of Ancient Buildings
37 Spital Square
London E1 6DY

Victoria and Albert Museum
Cromwell Road
London SW7 2RL

Victorian Society
1 Priory Gardens
Bedford Park
London W4 1TT

Wallpaper History Society
Victoria and Albert Museum
Cromwell Road
London SW7 2RL

**Sources of information in North America and Australia**

Australian Council of National Trusts
PO Box 1002
Civic Square
ACT 2608
Australia

Decorative Arts Society
c/o Brooklyn Museum
200 Eastern Parkway
Brooklyn
New York
NY 11238
USA

Metropolitan Museum of Art
5th Avenue at 82nd Street
New York
NY 10028
USA

National Trust for Historic Preservation (USA)
285 West Broadway
Suite 400
New York
NY 10013
USA

Society of Architectural Historians
1232 Pine Street
Philadelphia
PA 19107
USA

In the USA and Canada many communities have local historical societies whose members are very knowledgeable and who can offer invaluable information and advice.

The following are examples of medieval and Gothic Revival architecture that are open to the public. These are selected with an emphasis on domestic architecture, particularly where appropriate interiors and furnishings remain.

### Chapter 1: Gothic Forms and Gothic Sensibilities

Gothic abbeys, churches and cathedrals abound in England and northern France. The Loire Valley is famous for its late medieval and Renaissance châteaux, while Ireland and Wales are especially rich in medieval castles. The largest castle in western Europe is at Caerphilly in Wales.

**Museums:** The following are especially strong in holdings of medieval objects and decorative art:

The Cluny Museum, Paris, France. Contains an outstanding collection of medieval decorative art.

The Victoria and Albert Museum, London, England. Contains medieval decorative art and furniture.

The Metropolitan Museum of Art and its associated Cloisters Museum, New York City, USA. House a very important collection of medieval objects, decorative art, and architectural fittings.

### Domestic Architecture: Large Houses

Berkeley Castle, near Bristol, Gloucestershire. The oldest continuously inhabited castle in Britain, dating from the twelfth century.

The Bishop's Palace, Wells, Somerset. An impressive fortified and moated bishops' residence dating from the thirteenth to fifteenth centuries.

Bothwell Castle, Bothwell, Scotland. A large, well-preserved thirteenth-century castle.

Bramall Hall, Stockport, Cheshire. A large half-timbered late medieval house with nineteenth-century alterations. Contains late medieval wall paintings and Gothic Revival furniture by A W N Pugin and J G Crace.

Haddon Hall, Bakewell, Derbyshire. A rare survival of a large medieval house with original interiors and furnishings.

Leeds Castle, near Maidstone, Kent. A royal palace from the twelfth to the fifteenth centuries, Leeds is a moated castle containing medieval furnishings.

Little Moreton Hall, Congleton, Cheshire. Perhaps the classic example of a fifteenth-century timbered and moated manor house, with surviving wall paintings.

Penshurst Place, Tunbridge Wells, Kent. A large medieval house of several periods with medieval furnishings and interiors.

Skipton Castle, Yorkshire. A well-preserved medieval castle.

Smithills Hall, Bolton, Lancashire. Half-timbered manor house dating from the fifteenth century with a Great Hall and early period furnishings.

### Domestic Architecture: Small Houses

Dorney Court, Dorney, Buckinghamshire. A well-preserved small manor house of the fifteenth century, constructed of brick and timber and containing early furnishings.

House of Jacques Coeur, Bourges, France. The impressive Late Gothic stone townhouse of a wealthy financier.

Ightam Mote, Ivy Hatch, Kent. A moated medieval manor house, recently opened to the public, with an exhibition on building conservation.

The Manor House, Donnington-le-Heath, Leicestershire. A rare survival of a thirteenth-century manor house with restored furnishings and interiors.

Medieval Merchant's House, Southampton, Hampshire. A restored, half-timbered house of the 1290s with reproduction furnishings.

Paycocke's House, Coggeshall, Essex. A richly decorated late medieval merchant's townhouse of about 1500.

St Mary's House, Bramber, Sussex. A half-timbered manor house of the fifteenth century with sixteenth-century furnishings and 1890s Gothic alterations.

Tintagel Old Post Office, Tintagel, Cornwall. A small, stone house of the fourteenth century with its original hall. (The remains of the earlier castle are nearby.)

In addition, a wealth of late medieval town architecture can be found in the regions of eastern France and Belgium.

### Chapter 2: Picturesque Landscapes and Gothic Villas

Alnwick Castle, Alnwick, Northumberland. The large medieval seat of the Duke of Northumberland has Gothic designs by Robert Adam, who renovated it in the 1770s.

Arbury Hall, Nuneaton, Warwickshire. Originally a sixteenth-century house extensively remodelled in the Gothic style by Sir Roger Newdigate during the second half of the eighteenth century, with original interiors and furnishings.

Castle Ward, Co. Down, Northern Ireland. A 1760s house with a Gothic garden facade and some interiors in the Gothic style.

Claydon House, Middle Claydon, Buckinghamshire. Among its varied interiors is a 1770s Gothic room by the carver Luke Lightfoot, containing an interesting mix of medieval and Islamic elements.

Culzean Castle, Maybole, Scotland. Robert Adam castellated and remodelled the medieval remains during the 1770s, but the interiors are neo-classical.

Glin Castle, Glin, Co. Limerick, Ireland. A delightful example of eighteenth-century Gothic in Ireland.

Inverary Castle, Inverary, Scotland. An eighteenth-century turreted castle on the site of the medieval seat of the Duke of Argyll.

Lacock Abbey, Lacock, Wiltshire. An extremely interesting eighteenth-century Gothic house remodelled from a fine thirteenth-century abbey, with extensive medieval remains, including a cloister.

Milton Manor, Milton, Oxfordshire. A seventeenth-century house with a very fine eighteenth-century Gothic library and chapel built in the 1760s for a Catholic supporter of the Stuart cause.

Rousham House, Steeple Aston, Oxfordshire. William Kent's 1730s battlementing and Gothic garden monuments survive, along with a 1760s Gothic library by John Roberts.

Stonor Park, Stonor, Oxfordshire. A late medieval house of several periods whose Recusant family commissioned a Gothic Hall and chapel during the 1770s.

Strawberry Hill, Twickenham, Middlesex. The most famous of the eighteenth-century Gothic Revival monuments. Horace Walpole's house can be viewed, although his collections and furnishings have been dispersed.

### Chapter 3: Romantic Gothic: Abbeys and Castles

Arundel Castle, Arundel, Sussex. An enormous medieval castle with early and late nineteenth-century alterations in the Gothic style.

Ashridge Park, Berkhamstead, Hertfordshire. This large Regency Gothic house by James Wyatt, with assistance from Jeffry Wyatville, can sometimes be viewed by arrangement with the Ashridge Management College.

Auckland Castle, Bishop Auckland, Co. Durham. The residence of the Bishops of Durham since the twelfth century, with a Hall altered by James Wyatt in the Gothic style.

Belvoir Castle, Leicestershire. The Regency Gothic seat of the Duke of Rutland designed by James Wyatt on a Norman site. Medieval jousting tournaments are held on occasion.

Blairquhan Castle, Straiton, Maybole, Scotland. An unusual example of a Regency-period Gothic mansion in Scotland.

Hohenschwangau, Bavaria, Germany. A medieval hunting lodge of the Bavarian ruling family that was

Gothicized during the 1820s. Its interiors and furniture remain intact. Hohenschwangau was influenced by the castellated architecture of Regency England.

Lee Priory, Kent. A small installation from James Wyatt's Lee Priory Library of the 1780s is on view in the Victoria and Albert Museum, London.

Palacio da Pena, Sintra, Portugal. Essentially a romantic castle of the 1840s and 50s with a 'Manueline' Gothic exterior designed by the consort of Maria II.

Windsor Castle, Windsor, Berkshire. The medieval residence of the British monarchs. Much of the Gothic remodelling by James Wyatt and Jeffry Wyatville remains.

## Chapter 4: Pattern Books and Villas

These include some noteworthy American and Irish examples:

Ayesha Castle, Killiney, Co. Dublin, Ireland. An 1840s Gothic castle with some original features, although it was damaged by fire in the 1920s.

Carrigglas Manor, Co. Longford, Ireland. The house was built c1840 by an architect trained in the firm of Robert Adam.

Ever Rest, Hastings-on-Hudson, New York, USA. A late 1830s wooden cottage in 'carpenter's Gothic', the artist Jasper Cropsey added his own studio in the Gothic style c1885.

Kingscote, Newport, Rhode Island, USA. An 1830s Gothic villa designed by Richard Upjohn as a summer house for a wealthy businessman, subsequently enlarged.

Lyndhurst, Tarrytown, New York, USA. First built as a modest Gothic villa known as Knoll in the 1830s by Alexander Jackson Davis, and then enlarged by him during the 1860s to form the present Gothic Revival house.

Slane Castle, Co. Meath, Ireland. A late eighteenth-century example of James Wyatt's castellated style that influenced a number of early nineteenth-century Irish castles.

Tullynally Castle, Castlepollard, Co. Westmeath, Ireland. In the 1840s Richard Morrison enlarged upon the earlier Gothic Revival architecture of Francis Johnston.

'The Wedding Cake House', Kennebunkport, Maine USA. A classically designed colonial house was encased in wooden Gothic mouldings during the 1850s to bring the design up to date.

'Carpenter's Gothic' churches abound in upstate New York, New England, and Atlantic Canada. Two outstanding examples dating to the 1830s can be found in Machias and East Machias, Maine, near the Canadian border.

## Chapter 5: Gothic Archaeology and Gothic Propriety

Abbotsford, Melrose, Scotland. Remodelled during the second quarter of the nineteenth century in the 'Scottish Baronial' style by Walter Scott, with original furnishings intact.

Albury Park, near Guildford, Surrey. One of the few smaller country houses associated with A W N Pugin.

Alton Towers, Alton, Staffordshire. The ruined Regency Gothic house with partially extant 1840s interiors by A W N Pugin stands in the grounds of the famous amusement park.

Bryn Bras Castle, Llanrug, Wales. An archaeological 1830s revival of the Romanesque style, with original furnishings.

Eastnor Castle, near Ledbury, Herefordshire. A Regency Gothic castle by Robert Smirke with an impressive Gothic 'Saloon' by A W N Pugin and J G Grace remaining from c1850.

Government House, Perth, Australia. An 1860s Jacobean building with Gothic furniture designed by J G Grace, working in the Pugin manner. (Limited access.)

Knebworth House, Knebworth, Hertfordshire. Essentially a late medieval house with exterior alterations in the nineteenth century. The 1840s Gothic interiors by J G Grace were

removed except for the State Drawing Room and two antechambers. Original furnishings survive.

Lismore Castle, Co. Waterford, Ireland. A W N Pugin and J G Grace remodelled Lismore in the Gothic style in the middle of the nineteenth century. Original furnishings remain.

Palace of Westminster, Westminster, London. Limited access to the interiors is possible. The complex includes a medieval Great Hall, A W N Pugin interiors of the 1840s, and the 1950s Gothic of Giles Gilbert Scott in the rebuilt House of Commons.

## Chapter 6: Gothic Reform and Gothic Fantasy

All Saints' Church, Margaret Street, London. The earliest example of 1850s polychromatic Gothic is found in this richly decorated church by William Butterfield.

Biltmore, Asheville, North Carolina. An enormous example of the 'Chateau Gothic' of Richard Morris Hunt, who designed the house in the 1880s for the Vanderbilt family.

Canadian Parliament Buildings, Ottawa, Canada. Impressive despite an early twentieth-century rebuilding. Limited access is possible.

Cardiff Castle, Cardiff, Wales (and Castell Coch, nearby). The seat and summer house, respectively, of the Marquess of Bute form the most complete example of the work of William Burges, who remodelled the medieval castle during the 1860s and 70s. The outstanding interiors and furnishings remain intact.

Castle Drogo, near Chagford, Devon. An imposing and original early twentieth-century interpretation of castellated architecture by Edwin Lutyens.

Château Pierrefonds, Picardy, France. Impressive rebuilding of a late medieval fortified castle with lavish furnishings and interiors by Eugène Viollet-le-Duc dating to the 1860s.

Cragside House, Rothbury, Northumberland. Begun in the 1860s by Richard

Norman Shaw, with a mixture of revived half-timbering and castellated architecture, with original furniture.

Knightshayes Court, near Tiverton, Devon. 'Muscular Gothic' architecture by William Burges with 1870s Gothic interiors by J D Grace.

The Natural History Museum, South Kensington, London. The most famous example of the large, boldly modelled public buildings by Alfred Waterhouse during the 1870s and 1880s.

Neuschwanstein, Bavaria, Germany. The ultimate fantasy Gothic castle by a team of theatrical designers working for Ludwig II of Bavaria. The castle was unfinished at the time of his mysterious death in 1885.

Oxford University Museum, Oxford. The 1850s polychromy and naturalistic detail of the Museum, by an Irish team, is considered to be an embodiment of the ideas of John Ruskin.

Princeton University, Princeton, New Jersey, USA. Ralph Cram designed a Graduate College and University Chapel in a crisp, precise Gothic of the 1920s.

Trinity College, Hartford, Connecticut, USA. The original buildings of the college were designed by William Burges in the nineteenth century.

Ukraine Institute, New York City, USA. A richly ornamented Flamboyant Gothic townhouse by Richard Morris Hunt for a member of the Stuyvesant family c1900. The only Gothic interior is the stair hall.

University of Toronto, Toronto, Canada. University College was designed in 'muscular Gothic' by the team of Cumberland and Storm during the 1860s. Giles Gilbert Scott designed a mid-twentieth-century Chapel for Trinity College in the Gothic style.

Wightwick Manor, Wolverhampton, West Midlands. A late nineteenth-century black and white timbered house by Philip Webb with interiors by Morris and Co. showing some influence of the Gothic Revival.

Disney, Walt 221, *221*, 224
doorcases *110*, *177*, *211*
Dower House, Northumberland 224
Downing, Andrew Jackson 101, 113-17, *115*, *118*, 119, 120, 126, 170
Downton Castle, Herefordshire 72, 74
*The Dream of Guillaume de Loris 34*
dressers *145*, *171*
Duban, Felix *26*
Dunois, Counts of 33
Durham Cathedral *22*, 23

Early English Gothic 29, *30*, *31*, 87, 88, 110, 119-20, 188, *216*
Early Gothic 26, 29
Eastlake, Charles 202, *203*, 229
Eastnor Castle, Herefordshire 95, 167-9, *168*, *169*, 182-3
Eaton Hall, Cheshire 88, 95-8, *98*, *99*, 105, 114, 194, *199*
Ecclesiology Movement 176
Edgehill, Warwickshire 51
Edward II, King of England 69
Eglinton, Earl of 140, *140*
Eglinton Tournament 140, *140*
Eliot, George *53*, 55
Elizabeth I, Queen of England 141
Elliot brothers *80*
Elvills, Englefield Green, Berkshire *105*
Ely Cathedral 82
encaustic tiles *29*, *136*, 164, *164*
Ericstan, Tarrytown, New York *119*
Esher Place, Surrey 45-6, 60, 64
Evelyn, John 14
Exeter Cathedral 26, 183, *226-7*

Farey, Cyril *225*
Farquhar, Mr 89
Ferrey, Benjamin 17, 143, 146, 152, 170-3
Fish-keeper's Cottage, Port Logan, Scotland *103*
Fitzwilliam Museum, Cambridge *108*
Flamboyant Gothic 26-9, 33, 34, *37*, 69, *171*, *173*, 179, *181*, 182, *211*
Fonthill Abbey, Wiltshire 80, 82-9, *83-5*, *87*, 94, 95, *109*, 114, 133, *136*, 137
Fonthill Splendens, Wiltshire 83-4, 86
Fredericton Cathedral, New Brunswick, Canada 186
Freemantle, W H *105*
Fuller, Thomas 194

furniture 105-6
  bookcases *173*
  Burges's designs 216-18
  cabinets *204*, *208*, *213*
  chairs 64, *65*, *81*, *106*, *147*
  cradles *202*
  Davis's designs 120
  dressers *145*, *171*
  Gothic 34-5
  Pugin's designs 143-5, 146-9, *147*, *152*, *169*, *173*, 201
  Reformed Gothic 198
  settles 205, *206*
  sideboards *201*
  Street's designs 201-2
  tables *106*, *152*, *169*

garden structures 44, *44*, 48, 49-51
gardens, landscape 44-5
Gardiner, Richard 120
Gaudí Antonio 221
Gayfere, Thomas 80, 91
*Gentleman's Magazine* 79, 132
George III, King of England 79, 81, 93, *94*
George IV, King of England 93-4, 143
Gibbs, James 48, *48*
Glen Ellen, Maryland 117
Glin, 25th Knight of *74*
Glin Castle, County Limerick *74*
Gloucester Cathedral *14*, *15*, 31, 45, 82, *83*, 87
Gothic novels 19-20, 58, 67, 74, 84, 88, 138-40
Gothic Survival 36, 44, 224
Gothic Temple, Painshill, Surrey *47*
Gothic Temple, Shotover, Oxfordshire 44, 46
Gothic Temple, Stowe, Buckinghamshire 48, *48*
Gothic Villa, Regents Park, London *229*
Graham, James Gillespie *80*
'The Grange', Ramsgate, Kent 146, *149*
Graves, Lord *104*
Gray, Thomas 64, 66, 67
Great Exhibition (1851) 9, *152*, 169-70, *170*
Great Woolstone parsonage, Buckinghamshire 188
Grosvenor, Lord *98*
Gyfford, E 102, *102*, 103-4, 105, 106, 119

Haarlem, Netherlands 14
Hackney, London *198*
Hagley, Worcestershire 51, *68*
Haig, Axel *212*
Halfpenny, William *46*, *51*
Hall, Sir James 109, *112*, *113*
Hallett, William 64, *65*
Hamilton, Lady 86
Hampton Court, Herefordshire 38, 137
Hampton Lucy, Warwickshire 133-4
Hanbury Tracy, Charles (1st Baron Sudeley) 135, 189
  Hampton Court, Herefordshire 137, 138
  Palace of Westminster, London 137, 138
  Toddington Manor, Gloucestershire 130-3, *130-2*, 138
Hardman, John *148*, 164-7, *164*, 169, *169*, 179, 180
Harland and Fisher *3*
Hawksmoor, Nicholas *33*, *38*, 41
Hawthorne, Nathaniel 164
Henry III, King of England *29*, 41
Henry VIII, King of England 162
Henry of Reyns 29
Herrik, J *119*
Herter Brothers 208
Heywood, County Laois *73*
High Church Movement 186
Hiorne, William *51*
Hitchcock, Henry Russell 196
Hittorf, Jacques-Ignace 183
Hodson, George 126
Hodson, Sir Richard 126
Hoffman, Julius *221*
Hohenschwangau, Bavaria, Germany *221*
Holbein, Hans 66
Holland and Sons *201*
Hollar, Wencelaus 65
Holly, H Hudson 208-11
Holly Village, Highgate, London 194-6, *195*
Hollybrooke, County Wicklow 126
Hornsey, London *198*
House for James McConnochie, Park Place, Cardiff *212*
House of Lords *163*, 164, *164*
Hudson River Valley 117
Hulne Park, Northumberland *68*
Hunt, T F 111

Hussey, R W *108*

International Exhibition (1862) 201, 211, 212
Inverary Castle, Argyllshire 48-9
Irving, Washington 117
Islamic style 72, 109, 191, *208*, *210*

Jantzen, Hans 14
Janyns, Robert *29*
Jewitt, O *149*
John, King of England 48
Johnston, Francis *70*, *74*, *92*, *93*
Jones, George Noble 120
Jones, Owen *182*

Kames, Lord 48
Keene, Henry *51*, *53*, 55, 58, 66, 79
Kelly, Felix 224
Kenilworth Castle, Warwickshire 140-1
Kent, William 44-8, 58, 60
Kerr, Robert 191-3, 212
Kew Gardens, Surrey 69
Kew Palace, Surrey 93
King, William 120
Kingscote, Newport, Rhode Island 120, *123*
Knebworth House, Hertfordshire *167*
Knight, Richard Payne 72, 74, 111, 119
Knightshayes Court, Devon *216*
Knoll, Tarrytown, New York 117-23, *121*

Lacock Abbey, Wiltshire *49*, 52, *223*
Lacroux, J *196*, *197*
*The Lady and the Unicorn* tapestries *36*
Lainé, M 96
Lamb, E B 119
Landi, Gaetano *107*
landscape gardens 44-5
Langley, Batty 44, 45, *49*, *51*, 124, *127*, 224
  *Ancient Architecture Restored and Improved* 36-8, *40*, *41*, *44*, *46*, 52, 63
  influence 9, 51, 66, *68*, *71*, 72, *124*
Langley, Major 123-4
Laon Cathedral, Normandy 26
Lassus, Jean *26*
Latrobe, Benjamin 117
Law Courts, London 189, *190*
Lawrence, Richard 70
Lawrence, Sir Thomas 92-3
Le Viste family *36*